RESTAURANT
DESIGN

*Designing, Constructing & Renovating A
Food Service Establishment*

By Sharon L. Fullen

The Food Service Professional's Guide To:

Restaurant Design Designing, Constructing &
Renovating A Food Service Establishment: 365 Secrets
Revealed

Atlantic Publishing Group, Inc. Copyright © 2003
1210 SW 23rd Place
Ocala, Florida 34474
800-541-1336
352-622-5836 - Fax

www.atlantic-pub.com - Web Site
sales@atlantic-pub.com E-mail

SAN Number :268-1250

International Standard Book Number: 0-910627-24-X

Library of Congress Cataloging-in-Publication Data

Fullen, Sharon L.
Designing, constructing & renovating your restaurant : 365
secrets revealed / by Sharon L. Fullen.
p. cm. -- (The food service professionals guide to ; 14)
Includes bibliographical references and index.
ISBN 0-910627-24-X (pbk. : alk. paper)
1. Restaurants--Design and construction.   I. Title. II.
Title:Designing, constructing, and renovating your
restaurant. III. Series.
TX945.F85 2002
647.95'068'2--dc21
2002011170

Printed in Canada

Book layout and design by Meg Buchner of Megadesign
www.mega-designs.com • e-mail: megadesn@mhtc.net

CONTENTS

7. BACK-OF-THE-HOUSE

8. EQUIPMENT

INTRODUCTION

Whether you are pursuing your dream of owning a small ethnic restaurant or expanding your popular nightspot, you'll need to devote a significant portion of your financial resources and personal energy. This book provides you with practical tips and useful ideas to help you create a successful new restaurant or expand and revitalize your current restaurant.

Hopefully, before a single hammer is lowered, you'll have used this book to:

- Guide you through the critical research and preplanning stages and establish your personal and business goals.

- Understand the relationship between your customers and employees and your restaurant's design, décor and food.

- Assist you in developing a solid business plan to establish your goals while satisfying the needs of your partners, employees, investors and bankers.

- Assemble a team of professionals (real estate brokers, designers, contractors and consultants) ready to share their expertise and create a synergy for success.

No book can address every issue that might arise while building, redecorating or renovating a restaurant. Our goal is to prepare you to ask the right questions, make the right decisions and feel comfortable with the process. Here we have addressed dozens of important topics and how they affect your customers, your employees and your pocketbook.

We wish you much success as you realize your dream...

CHAPTER ONE

RESEARCH & PLANNING

Exploring Yourself

A little self-analysis can be good for the soul - and for your business. Exploring your interests, expectations and the commitments (financial, physical and emotional) necessary to meet your entrepreneurial goals is what we call the pre-planning stage.

Operating a restaurant is hard work and the failure rate is, unfortunately, significant. However, realizing your dream can be an exceptionally rewarding endeavor; personally and professionally. The ingredients for success go well beyond an exquisite pasta primavera or a succulent prime rib. They are a complex blend of passion, vision, risk taking and business acumen. Your clarity of vision will help you write your business plan, sell your concept to lenders and potential investors and communicate your desires and needs to architects, contractors, designers and suppliers. Explore the following issues:

- **Close your eyes.** Can you see your dream restaurant? Is the dining area filled with cheerful conversations and bustling staff? Can you smell the enticing aromas drifting from the kitchen? Do your taste buds tingle when you think of your specialty dish? These images all represent your passion.

- **Think carefully.** Take a few hours of uninterrupted time to think over your personal and financial reasons for committing your "nest egg," taking on a partner or tying yourself to a long-term loan.

- **Create a list of the positives and negatives**. Every venture has risks (negatives), but the positives should outweigh them. If your entrepreneurial spirit isn't damped by the potential risks, your next step is to give your vision a voice.

- **Determine what talents you can bring to the process.** Do you have great color sense or are you color-blind? Do you want to write a check and let the professionals handle the details? Or do you want to be consulted on every detail from the front door to the walk-in freezer?

A Restaurant Serves More than Food

As a restaurateur, you aren't just serving food, you are fulfilling your customers' needs. Whether you own a pizza parlor filled with video games or a mahogany-paneled dinner house, your restaurant is where people will be emotionally and physically nourished, entertained, stimulated, relaxed, pampered and satisfied.

Your construction and design decisions go well beyond what's on the menu. The popular Chuck E. Cheese's franchise chain and Wolfgang Puck's Spago restaurants both serve pizza, but no one could confuse them. Consider the following:

- **Ambiance.** You need to create a physical environment that exactly meets the needs of your customers. You'll want to decide what type of environment you'll create when building, decorating or renovating your restaurant.

- **Creative ideas.** Construction and design require-ments and costs are directly affected by what you want to offer your customers. Also, what will your restaurant mean to your customers? Here are some creative concepts to help stimulate your thinking.

Do you want to...
- Attract multigenerational families for family gatherings, or provide teens with a place to hangout?
- Catch only the lunchtime crowd or be open 24/7?
- Feed people in a hurry, or create a cozy place to linger with after-dinner drinks and cigars?
- Delight dozens of kids celebrating birthdays, or cater to adults only?
- Share your native country's cuisine, or serve All-American cafeteria fare?
- Present elegantly plated meals, or feature an all-you-can-eat buffet?
- Have a mellow jazz trio or a local rock band entertaining on Saturday night?

Create Your Vision

Your restaurant is more than a building with stoves, tables and chairs - it is a reflection of your personality, your love of food and your desire to share your passion. Designing and constructing a restaurant is a cooperative effort. One way to build resourceful allies and working partnerships is to share your dream with them. Sure, you'll be paying for their services, but developing deeper relationships empowers them "go the extra mile" in realizing your vision. An important part of starting a new business or revitalizing an existing one is to have well-developed ideas and established goals. Below are some creative activities to help you visualize your new or revitalized restaurant. Make it a reality! Take those important first steps:

- **Develop your complete daily menu.** Many future decisions will be based on knowing what you'll be serving how and why you are serving it.

- **Samples.** Acquire samples of your chosen dinnerware, flatware, tablecloths, napkins and tabletop items (vases, advertising, napkin holders, etc.). Pick up paint swatches and material samples from your local home improvement center, tile store, fabric store or paint store.

- **Portfolio.** Build a "vision portfolio" which holds your sketches, ideas, notes and decorative swatches.

- **Get some ideas.** Clip design ideas from trade publications or home improvement magazines.

- **Rough sketches.** Make sketches (as detailed as your skills allow) of your dream restaurant.

- **Gather decorative pieces that symbolize your theme.** Such things as antique posters, a cowboy hat or a wine label can serve as design focal points from which to build a decorative theme.

- **Write a one-minute "elevator pitch."** If you found yourself in an elevator with a wealthy investor, how would you describe your vision (and secure the cash) in the time it takes to travel up 20 floors? Show your passion while emphasizing the tangible benefits.

- **Write a one-page marketing plan.** How will you announce your new restaurant? What will make your place different and successful?

- **Write a formal business plan.** For more information, read the section "Writing a Business Plan."

What's on the Menu?

Your general and specific menu offerings and presentation style directly impact your equipment needs, space requirements, layout and décor. The needs of an elegant dinner house are significantly different to those of a take-out burger palace. By developing a full menu, you'll be able to start building lists of your desires and needs. Below are the some ideas to think over as you create a typical menu for each mealtime you're open - breakfast, lunch, dinner and late night.

- **Make note of all your non-food needs for each food service step.** This will help you determine the specific equipment, layout and budget you'll need to create a good work environment while serving meals in a timely and cost-effective manner.

  Include notes on the following:
  - **Prep** - Tools, equipment and workspace requirements.
  - **Storage** - Pantry, refrigeration and freezer requirements.
  - **Cooking** - Equipment, environmental (lighting, ventilation, drainage, etc.) and workflow requirements.
  - **Serving** - Serving bowls, utensils and equipment (carts, warming lamps, ice buckets, etc.) needs.

- **Play to the stereotypical or break the mold.** Some food genres conjure up strong visual images - Mexican restaurants with pinatas and sombreros, or Chinese restaurants,with fiery dragons and golden Buddhas. Restaurant décor can go beyond the stereotypical even in ethnic restaurants. Not all restaurants are theme restaurants, but all restaurants should have a unifying theme (look) that accentuates the food served.

- **Choose how you will present your food.** Your signature dish formally served on white bone china or dished up on paper plates offers styling cues that affect your entire décor. Elegant china place settings speak of traditional styling, while paper plates might remind one of funky low-back chairs and Formica tables.

- **Determine how your diners will be served.** Will diners serve themselves at a salad bar or will you have tableside preparation? Will people pick up their meals at a counter, or will a server deliver each meal personally?

- **Think about the future now.** Your menu could change up to 50 percent over the first six months of operation. Think about potential revisions and select equipment and designs that offer flexibility.

Research and Analysis

Researching your new concept and construction plans and developing feasibility studies and analysis doesn't sound like much fun. However, not doing your homework can create costly mistakes. Here are some helpful suggestions on the research and analysis process. In order to prepare your business plan, establish your profit potential and make purchasing decisions, you'll first need to gather various types of data and information on demographics. Bear in mind the following:

Demographic data you'll need to know:
- **The local population.** Are there enough potential customers?
- **Their economic status.** Can they afford $25 a plate?
- **Their lifestyles.** Are potential customers mostly singles or single parents?
- **Their buying habits.** Do they limit dining out to weekends and holidays?

Demographic sources.
Gather demographic data from trade organizations, government agencies and your commercial real estate broker. Below are some trade associations that provide free or low-cost data:

- **Contact the National Restaurant Association** for information on your specific state associations, www.restaurant.org or 800-424-5156.

- **The National Bar and Restaurant Association** at www.bar-restaurant.com or 866-368-3753.

- **The National Bed and Breakfast Association** at www.nbba.com.

- **Travel Association of America** at www.tia.org or 202-408-8422.

- **Hospitality Sales and Marketing Association International** at www.hsmai.org or 202-789-0089.

- **Don't forget to ask about tourist data.** Contact local business development organizations, chambers of commerce and tourist bureaus.

- **Hire an expert.** Web-based services, such as Any Site atwww.anysite.com/restaurant.htm, sell information and handle research.

Visit your local library or online databanks.
Library. Ask about free research assistance from trained librarians:
- Demographics USA (ZIP edition) - market statistics

- Lifestyle market analyst: Standard Rate and Data Service - look under "gourmet cooking/fine foods" and cross-reference market, lifestyle, consumer

- Standard and Poor's Industry Surveys

Online.
- www.ameristat.org

- www.quickfacts.census.gov/qfd/index.html

- www.searchbug.com/reference/demographics.asp

•The San Francisco Public Library Web site at www.sfpl4.sfpl.org/btdir/rest2.htm. There's lots of valuable information here, even if you aren't local.

Visit Your Competition

An important part of selecting your concept and determining its potential success is to study the competition. Does the neighborhood need another pizzeria or do steak-lovers have to travel miles for a good filet mignon? Remember, these are research expeditions to help you create your restaurant's niche, learn from others' experiences and determine your potential for success. Here are some suggestions to help you scout the competition:

- **Mark your potential location on a street map.** Draw a circle around the mark - for "walking" neighborhoods, a six-block radius should be enough; for "driving" neighborhoods, start with a quarter mile. This is your initial study area. You can always expand your research territory based on how far you believe people will travel for a meal out.

- **Visit every business that serves food or drinks,** including grocery stores, fast-food restaurants, bars and cafeterias. This is your potential competition. Trips to a busy supermarket salad bar may reveal that tired office workers just want to get home and feed the kids. Your noisy, fun sports-bar concept could be a mismatch.

- **Dine at your direct competition;** establishments that feature similar menus, themes or serve your model customer.

- **Be a restaurant critic.** Make notes of what works and what doesn't.

- **Look around the room.** Even if they serve the same food genre, do they serve the same crowd?

- **How do the patrons interact with the physical surroundings?** Do people appear relaxed in the chairs? Are the booths too big for the little ones? Do teens spend time at the video games?

- **Think about joining in.** Notice how there seems to be a fast-food store on every corner. This isn't poor planning but a belief that impulse dining means being within reach when the urge strikes. A burger joint across from a taco stand that is next to take-out fish-and-chips means that mom and dad can please everyone in the car!

Use your research to confirm your chosen concept and to. . .
- Write a powerful business plan that convinces lenders and investors of your potential.

- Develop your marketing campaigns.

Who Is Your Ideal Customer?

A critical part of the planning stage is to determine who your audience is and how to please them. Knowing this will help you:

- **Serve their food preferences.** Hearty breakfasts for the construction crowd or latte and muffin for the busy secretary.

- **Be conveniently located** to home, work and/or play.

- **Be available when they have the urge.** A coffee shop open at 6 a.m. and a bar until the wee hours.

- **Create an appropriate, comfortable environment.** Dirty work jeans and washable vinyl booths or the classic black cocktail dress and elegant marble floors.

- **Visualize a target customer.** Create a customer

model. By establishing a perfect fictional "repeat" customer, you'll have a "target" audience in mind when developing your concept. Don't forget that your ideal customer may be a man or woman, teens, an elderly couple, a small group or a family unit. Your real customers will be a combination; however, trying to appeal to everyone is a losing proposition.

- **Prepare a list of basic characteristics,** such as sex, age and where they live. Continue to add greater detail about the diners, such as dress, education, career and marital status. Now develop a character with likes and dislikes, dreams and desires. Visualize this person's process in coming to your restaurant. Does he or she arrive by car from a nearby mall, walk over from an office building or drop by after long road trip? Who would this customer's dinner companions be? Your fictional diner rarely eats alone. Who will be joining him or her?

- **Determine the "true" decision maker.** Your target customer may not pay the check. Restaurants that cater to tots are rarely the first choice for an adults-only evening. Likewise, the secluded booth in the back isn't a draw to a toddler.

- **Consider whether your restaurant should cater to the decision- aker or offer benefits to multiple audiences.** Again, remember that trying to satisfy everyone means you probably won't satisfy anyone.

Location, Location, Location

Many factors affect where people choose to dine. But one of the most important is location. Location considerations break down into three categories: Physical - is there enough physical space for your operations? Are you conveniently located for customers? Emotional - does your location feel safe and comfortable? Would your ideal customer think of looking here for your food genre and service style? Need - does the neighborhood need another restaurant of your type? Are there enough potential customers nearby? The following suggestions will help you select the best location for your food service venture:

- **Drive around the neighborhood,** visit local businesses and nearby competition. Observe traffic volume and patterns during meal times.

- **Look for complementary businesses** that draw hungry people into the area. Examples of complementary busi-nesses are movie houses, department stores, schools and office buildings. Take advantage of the crowds they attract.

- **Be easy to find** (deliberately or accidentally). Visibility is "free" marketing to people walking or driving by. Don't rely on a few signs to bring them to your "hidden" door. Diners often pass by dozens of times before deciding to join you.

- **Ask your real estate broker to direct you to "successful" business areas** and restaurant-friendly landlords.

- **Avoid places where other restaurants have failed.** This unwritten rule factors in multiple reasons a restaurant can fail; however, it has proven to be true time and time again.

- **Review the location for future needs.** Expanding your facility or moving can be costly and create new "location" problems, including losing hard-earned regulars.

- **Does the space provide for sufficient seating?** Remember, seats = dollars. Use a cost-per-square-foot-per-seat factor when considering rent/lease or construction costs.

- **Think of busy areas that lack food service** and **17**

meet their needs! Be open when they are there (early breakfast or late-night cocktails), be closed when they aren't, and serve food how they want it (to-go quick or resort leisure).

Feasibility Studies and Analysis

No restaurant owner starts an endeavor thinking she'll fail. However, many do. The very traits that make you a prime candidate to own your own restaurant - independence, drive and a touch of ego - are also those that make you less likely to put ample effort and time into research and analysis. By thoroughly exploring your immediate and long-term profit potential and your financial needs during startup and other survival periods, you'll be increasing your odds for success. It's time to put some numbers together for your business plan. Whether you commission extensive studies and analysis or get out your own calculator, you'll need to undertake some feasibility studies. Here are some helpful hints on preparing or commissioning feasibility studies.

- **Grasp the basics.** There are two types of feasibility studies:
  - **Marketing feasibility studies** define and study your customers, your competition and your community.
  - **Financial feasibility studies** ask and answer the hard questions in dollars and cents: "How much will it cost?", "What are my projected income and expenses?", "Can it be profitable?", "Do I need more financial backing to survive until the business becomes successful?", "Is it worth the effort?"

- **Review a sample study.** The Small Business Development Center operated by the University of North Carolina has a broad-range study posted at www.sbtdc.org/research/restaurant.pdf.

- **Research.** Read the sections "Visit the Competition," "Who's Your Ideal Customer?" and "Get Out Your Calculator" for more research ideas. Purchase the National Restaurant Association's do-it-yourself manual, Conducting a Feasibility Study for a New Restaurant. To order, call 800-424-5156 ext. 5375.

- **Hire a consultant.** Check Yahoo for restaurant & food service management consulting firms or the Food Service Consultants Society at www.fcsi.org, 502-583-3783, for specialists.

Get Out Your Calculator

Get out your calculator and do some calculations on your own. This can be hard to do, especially if you haven't opened yet. But speaking with local restaurateurs (even competitors are often willing to share basic information) can help you "guesstimate." Below are some helpful decision-making formulas.

- **Figure your projected income.** It's better to under-estimate slightly when projecting income.

- **Compute the number of guests you'll serve** each day for each meal period (breakfast, lunch and dinner). Multiply the number of seats by the number of turns and total all three for a guests per day figure.

- **Figure your total guests** per week (multiply guests per day by days open per week), per month (multiply guests per day by 30), and per year (multiply guests per month by 12).

- **Figure an average check**. Take a variety of meals (drink, appetizer, main course and dessert) and average the price of these. Multiply the number of guests by the average check to figure your projected income.

19

- **Figure your projected costs and expenses.**
  Calculate percentage-of-sales factors for food,
  beverage and staffing needs. Base these variables on
  your number of customers, industry averages and
  your own local research. Contact food and beverage
  suppliers for purchasing estimates. Ask peers for
  prevailing wage and benefit data.

- **Obtain the current National Restaurant
  Association's Industry Operations Report.** Visit
  their Web site at www.restaurant.org, or call 800-
  424-5156.

- **Compile costs** for operational expenses and
  overhead, such as insurance, utilities, equipment
  loans and rent.

- **Take a deep breath and subtract your projected
  costs and expenses from your projected income.**
  This significantly reduced number is your estimated
  gross profit.

- **Return on investment (ROI).** calculations are
  excellent decision-making tools and help balance out
  your enthusiasm in growing your business. Use
  these figures to determine whether remodeling costs
  of $85,000 to add 25 seats is a wise investment, or
  how long it will take to return a profit after spending
  $500,000 on a new restaurant. You're now ready to
  prepare your business plan's financial section.

Writing a Business Plan

No lender or potential investor would seriously consider
underwriting your project without a written business
plan. However, you may not realize how useful a business
plan can also be for you and your employees. A well-
thought-out plan is more than just some dry statistics and
financial mumbo-jumbo. A good business plan reflects

your desires and goals and sets everyone on a formal path to meet these. Successful entrepreneurs will tell you that the most important thing you can do is plan! Here are some business plan tips and reasons to take the time to put everything in writing:

- **Write it yourself.** The process of writing your plan is an opportunity to carefully think through your financial and staffing needs, define your restaurant's concept (theme) and prepare you for undergoing a major construction or renovation project. A sample plan can be found at www.virtualrestaurant.com/sample.htm.

- **Create a two-page written plan as a personal and professional goal-setting tool,** even if your needs don't require a lengthy, formal written presentation. This simple plan should outline your objective (what you wish to accomplish), define a course of action and set progress benchmarks.

- **Purchase a fill-in-the-blank business plan book** from your local bookstore. Or, investigate a popular software package like Business Plan Pro from Palo Alto Software to get you started. These guides will ask thought-provoking questions and help you organize your thoughts, gather research data and present it in a straightforward manner.

- **Check with your state's Small Business Development Center** and the Small Business Administration (SBA) at www.sba.gov. Or, try your local university for free or low-cost business-plan-writing classes. Besides learning how to write your plan, the discipline of attending a class can provide focus for busy entrepreneurs.

- **Hire a business communications specialist** to "spruce up" your plan. An experienced business plan writer can polish your presentation to dazzle bankers and investors.

- **Include employees in writing your plan.** This process builds strong partnerships while increasing employees' satisfaction. Their input can be invaluable and sharing your vision will increase your potential for success.

Should You Do it Yourself?

Some redecorating and minor remodeling projects are suitable for do-it-yourselfers. Painting an entryway can be an enjoyable, creative and cost-effective project for an entrepreneur. However, as a busy restaurateur, you may be "spending" too much on do-it-yourself projects. Here are a few thought-provokers to help you determine whether you should undertake the supervision and/or the actual work instead of hiring a professional:

- **Consider your prior experience.** Projects that require building permits and inspections should only be handled by the appropriate licensed professional.

- **Consider your skill level.** Be honest about the quality level you expect and your ability to deliver. Paying a professional to "fix" your work can be very costly.

- **How much time will it take?** Think back to your experience and skill level. Then estimate the project's do-it-yourself time and double it! Remember, distractions will happen, and projects can go awry.

- **Can you afford the retail cost?** Simple projects can often be accomplished within budget by paying retail. However, wholesale pricing, trade discounts and the purchasing skills of a professional can actually offset a considerable portion of the consultant's fee. Many decorative and construction products are only available to licensed professionals. The product selection and quality is often superior to anything available to a layperson.

- **Can you afford potential problems?** Acting as your own general contractor may seem cost effective. However, you'll be financially and legally responsible.

- **What is your time worth?** Your earnings may seem like minimum wage, but your true value to your restaurant, customers and employees may exceed the cost of hiring a professional.

- **What won't you be doing?** When calculating the labor cost of a do-it-yourself project, you should factor in the "cost" of what you won't be doing.

- **Don't assume you can't afford a professional.** Obtain at least two quotes before you dismiss the idea. Even if you choose to do it yourself, you may obtain valuable information on how the pro would approach the project.

Who Pays for What?

During construction or remodeling, you can be held financially liable for unpaid materials, labor or services under legal claims called construction, or mechanic, liens. Even if you have paid your contractor for these, it is your responsibility to see that purchases made on your behalf are paid. So, ask a few questions first:

- **What is a construction lien?** This is a legal claim meant to secure payment for goods or services used in the construction or renovation of your property. Paying your contractor does not absolve you from this lien - that's why you should take preemptive steps to protect yourself and your business. To learn more about construction liens, contact your local construction contractor board or speak with your attorney regarding laws in your state.

- **For what types of goods and services can I be held responsible for?** If your contractor does not pay subcontractors, employees, rental equipment firms or material suppliers, or make other legally required payments on your behalf, those who are owed money may file a lien against your property.

What can I do to protect my business ?

- **Always have a signed contract.** For larger projects, have an attorney review the provisions regarding paying for goods and services purchased on your behalf.

- **Call the Contractors Board** to confirm that your contractor has a current license in good standing.

- **Establish a periodic payment or progress payment schedule** based upon your ability to confirm that all related bills are paid.

- **Make checks jointly payable** to the contractor and supplier, or pay the supplier directly.

- **Request that your contractor post a performance bond** for the total project amount.

- **Establish an escrow account** to distribute funds to suppliers/creditors.

- **Obtain waivers** for the Right to Lien whenever possible.

- **Contact a title company** about obtaining a title policy that protects you from construction lien claims.

- **Read over any Notices of Right to Lien,** Consumer Notification Forms or other documentation provided by your contractor explaining your rights.

- **Prior to making any final payments, obtain written lien releases** from each of the contractors and materials suppliers.

CHAPTER TWO

BUILDING YOUR TEAM

Consult the Experts

Building a team of professionals, consultants and trade people is the foundation of your development project. Depending upon the nature and scope of your needs, you may require only one or two specialists, or you may work with six or seven team members. Each expert will handle specific aspects of the design, construction and equipping of your restaurant. Some will have multiple disciplines in which they can provide invaluable services and advice. Here are some suggestions to help you maximize your resources and develop a cohesive team:

- **Write a Request for Proposal** (RFP) that details your needs. A written RFP ensures that each service provider/vendor is "bidding" on your project based on the same facts. The more information you provide, the more accurate their response. Service providers/vendors can anticipate some of your needs, but they cannot read minds. If you're smart, you'll hire a take-charge food service consultant or project manager first and have him or her handle all the other RFPs.

- **Good consultants will give you a thorough and reflective proposal.** Review each proposal for an understanding of the scope of the project, suitable approaches and creative solutions, as well as fees and services to be provided.

- **Check references.** Their portfolios are impressive, and they say all the right things, BUT do they listen well, return calls promptly, meet deadlines and give projects their appropriate attention? Just like when hiring good employees, checking references is important.

- **Speak directly with people they have worked with (and for).** Talk to project managers, restaurant owners or managers and other decision-makers. Whenever possible, review similar projects they've completed.

- **Clarify any areas** of the proposal you are unsure of BEFORE signing a contract.

- **Treat your consultant respectfully.** Be prepared for meetings. Try not to waste this time. Keep the lines of communication open. Keep him in the loop.

How Consultants Get Paid

Consultants can be paid on an hourly basis, a fixed flat fee, a percentage above costs or a combination of these. Your job is to not overpay for services, but it is in your interest to pay fairly. Consultants who make a fair profit for their services will reward you with a partnership mentality. The following are some things to keep in mind when paying a consultant:

- **Save money by clearly defining a project** before having the consultant prepare a proposal. It is also critical that you understand and agree on what is to be "delivered." Miscommunications can mean costly delays, incomplete projects or an unsatisfactory completion.

- **Be prepared to handle consultants' fees.** How will expenses be billed? Will progress payments be requested for long-term projects? A retainer fee may be requested.

- **Clarify what additional expenses will be billed above base fees.** Out-of-pocket expenses, such as lodging, travel and shipping, are typically billed separately. The consultant's proposal should clearly spell these out.

For projects to be billed on an hourly basis:

- **Define the project clearly** and have the consultant give you a time estimate.

- **Set a billing maximum** if a more open-ended arrangement is agreed upon.

For fixed-fee projects:

- **Ask for proposals to include an estimate of time** required (in hours) to complete the project. Flat-fee billing may seem like a safe choice, but it can also mean you are overpaying for some services. The consultant typically pads the quote to cover unfore-seeable efforts that require additional hours.

For above-cost fees:

- **Choose this payment method for interior decorators, equipment engineers** or other consultant "shoppers." These consultants receive trade discounts and then charge you a percentage above their costs.

- **Verify that the "purchasing agent" is independent** and can offer you products from competitive manufacturers.

- **Free with purchase.** Avoid this arrangement if possible. As the saying goes, "You get what you pay for," which could be biased information, encourage-ment to purchase too much or too costly goods and a less-than-desired level of expertise.

How to Select Restaurant/Food Service Consultants

The title "food service consultant" covers a broad range of disciplines, ranging from research and analysis to design and purchasing. You may determine that one consultant or firm can handle your project, or you may require multiple specialists. A full-service firm can become your primary consultant and source additional independent consultants based upon your project needs.

- **Build a list of consultants** who specialize in food service consulting.

- **Ask other restaurant owners for referrals.** Did the consultant perform well and meet expectations and budgets?

- **Contact the Foodservice Consultants Society International** at www.fcsi.org, 502-583-3783.

- **Check the Yellow Pages** under "Restaurant Consultants."

- **Create a basic "job" description.** Decide which aspect of the project you wish for the consultant to be responsible. Will you need a written report or someone to work hands-on?

- **Speak with each consultant to narrow down your list to two or three candidates.** Some larger firms may have staff that can handle multiple needs; others may only meet one requirement. Listen to their concerns about your project and needs. Do they ask probing questions or do they spend the conversation trying to convince you just how great they are?

- **Ask to speak with whom you will be working with directly.** Will you be handed off to a less-experienced associate or will you be working with the owner? Can you communicate your ideas easily to this person? Is there good rapport?

- **Write a Request for Proposal (RFP)** that details your needs. A written RFP ensures that each consultant is "bidding" on your project based on the same facts. The more information you provide, the more complete and accurate a response you'll receive.

- **Request a written proposal from your finalists.** Along with their proposal and quote, you should receive background information, company brochures, samples (if appropriate) and references.

Commercial Real Estate Broker

Whether you're seeking to lease or purchase a commercial building or appropriately zoned land, a real estate broker should be hired to represent your interests. Securing a qualified commercial broker can save you hundreds of hours and thousands of dollars. Although you may not be paying your broker directly for his or her services, you are definitely paying for this service, as this "cost of doing business" impacts the seller's/lessor's asking price. A commercial broker's commission is substantial, so insist that you get your money's worth. Here are five tips to help you select the best agent for your needs.

1. **Find someone who values your time, listens to your needs and asks probing questions.** Many hours have been wasted looking at inadequate buildings or unaffordable properties by real estate representatives who don't listen or ask important questions.

2. **Don't rely on the seller's/lessor's representative.** Seek out your own broker to avoid conflicts of interest.

3. **Source out someone who specializes in restaurant properties in your community.** Hiring someone familiar with the local market can help you find properties that are just becoming available.

4. **Select someone who is experienced in lease negotiation.** Not all brokers handle real estate leasing. A good tenant representative can handle the entire negotiation process on your behalf. Based upon personal knowledge of the market, he or she can broker more favorable lease rates, improvement allowances, out clauses and other concessions.

5. **Hire someone with creativity and problem-solving skills.** Rarely will the perfect property be out there when you need it. Each restaurant and owner has different requirements. An agent who has a good grasp of your needs and thinks creatively can be invaluable.

Your Construction Team

Architect

An experienced architect can save you thousands in material and construction costs and avoid potential code and legal issues. Your architect is also an important source for recommendations on specialty consultants and contractors who can fulfill your project specifications. A rapidly expanding service is "design-build," where every aspect - from the planning stage to the grand opening - is handled by one firm.

- **Preplanning meeting.** Insist that the architect visit your site or building for a pre-planning session before you make a purchase or sign a lease. By having your architect evaluate the site for suitability, you can be assured that you will have sufficient square footage for your needs, determine potential construction costs or special needs, and review code compliance issues.

- **Choose design firms with restaurant/hospitality experience.** Designing a ten-story office building or mini-mall has no relation to creating a showplace restaurant or trendy nightclub. The complexity of a food service environment requires a specific knowledge of entertainment, food production and safety issues, as well as numerous government regulations.

- **In-house/subcontract.** Ask what work will be done in-house (by employees) and what will be subcontracted.

Contractors

If you have not chosen a design-build firm, you'll need to select a general contractor to oversee the construction and/or renovation. Your architect and food service consultant can give you referrals and share their personal experiences of potential candidates.

- **Start by reviewing your architect's recommendations.** There can be a real advantage in building a team where members have already worked together successfully.

- **Ask for referrals from other restaurant owners.** Ask them to share their real-world experiences. Did they exceed the budget? Did they show up on time? Were they attentive to detail?

- **Look beyond the contractor's portfolio.** Ask plenty of questions about his or her expertise, professionalism and financial stability.

- **Ask for and verify all trade and business licenses, permits, insurance and bonds.** See the following sections for additional construction trade information.

Your Business Team

Your business advisers and financial supporters play important roles in building or renovating your restaurant. If this is your first entrepreneurial experience, you'll want to seek out these essential support people early on.

Lawyer

In our litigious society, a businessperson's best friend can be a lawyer. Purchasing property, signing leases and hiring consultants and contractors can all have long-term legal, financial and personal ramifications:

- **Find a business lawyer before you need one** in order to avoid last-minute panics.

- **Submit all contracts and agreements for review** to avoid pitfalls.

- **Schedule a meeting** to discuss your business structure, personal asset protection and liability issues.

Accountant

New construction, remodeling and decorating projects all cost money - and frequently more than you'd like to spend. A good accountant can guide your financial decisions and help you prepare your business plan. If you don't have an accountant, hire one to:

- **Get your current personal and business finances in order.** Lenders and investors will look closely at these.

- **Understand what you can afford to spend for your project.** Determine what type of loan payment you can afford or savings plan you can implement.

- **Assist in locating an investor or borrowing money.** Accountants can help with completing forms, preparing for interviews and reviewing the financial section of your business plan.

- **Prepare financial feasibility reports.** These can help you determine your return on investment, profit potential and cash flow.

- **Analyze the true cost** of owning versus leasing or renting equipment; building versus renovating; and business structures (partnerships, S or C corporations, LLC).

- **Advise on the tax implications** for purchasing equipment, investing in renovations, expanding your business, etc.

Banker

Even though we are in the age of Web-based banks, it is still possible to develop a relationship with a local banker. Banks rarely grant construction loans for fledgling businesses. However, many do handle SBA-backed loans:

- **A banker can help you establish a line of credit** for immediate (pre-funding) needs. You'll have some out-of-pocket costs before financing or an investor is secured.

- **Ask for advice.** Some bankers have a small-business department that offers business classes and can review your business plan and direct you to alternative lenders or government-backed programs.

Leading Them All

Each team member will have his or her own priorities and agendas based upon their respective role. No matter how large or small your project, you must appoint a team leader to handle the three Cs - coordination, communication and compromise. The leader could be you, your food service consultant, your builder or a general contractor. Some projects may have more than one leader, depending upon the project size. A successful team leader needs to understand the overall project, be readily available, be well organized and have good people skills. Here are some leadership tips to help you create a strong development team:

- **Have a project party.** Invite service providers and vendors to a social evening to introduce everyone. Mix business with pleasure to develop strong working relationships.

- **Hold an orientation meeting** where plans, dreams and expectations are shared. Create an atmosphere where ideas are discussed, decisions are made and responsibilities are assigned.

- **Develop and share a project contact list.** Gather vital information such as contact names, personal and cell phone numbers and e-mail addresses.

- **Establish a desired contact method** and set urgency factors and required response times. Communication is crucial, but not all messages require an urgent response.

- **Schedule periodic and regular progress meetings.** Take notes and distribute critical information to all parties to reinforce schedules and agreements.

- **Establish the leader's authority and responsibility** (especially in making decisions in your absence).

- **Develop a central location for project information and messages:**
    - An in-house Web site (a great example can be found at www.gilbertconstruct.com/ProjectManagement.htm).
    - A Web-based project management service, such as construction-industry-specific sites

www.e-builder.net or www.myconstruction.com, or general project management sites, such as www.intranets.com or www.same-page.com.

- An office bulletin board, a voice-mail-based message system or an e-mail newsletter.

- **Send out progress reports** to keep priorities and schedules intact.

- **Understand that some situations will require a compromise.** Remember each project team member views an issue through the lens of his or her specialty. Their ideas and opinions may be in direct conflict with the needs and expectations of others. Listen and lead.

All Those Workers and No Work!

Undertaking any construction project requires an understanding of the nature of construction trades. While these are honorable professions, the majority of all consumer complaints are construction-related. Bear in mind the following about the nature of the construction trades:

- **There is a shortage of skilled laborers** within all areas of construction. During peak season, delays may be inevitable.

- **Language barriers.** Many construction workers are not native English-speakers or may not speak English at all.

- **Subcontractors frequently work on a per-piece basis.** They probably have multiple jobs going simultaneously and may have to work long days, weekends and holidays to earn a living.

- **Time management isn't a strong suit.** Don't be surprised when appointments aren't kept.

35

However, don't ignore these lapses in professionalism. Insist that schedules be met and appointments honored.

- **Being a talented finish carpenter doesn't mean you are a skilled businessperson.** Tradespeople are often self-employed. They often suffer from cash flow problems and limited business experience. Be diligent about the activities they undertake on your behalf.

Here are some practical ways to get the best from your contractors, installers and suppliers:

- **Obtain their state license numbers.** Before hiring any contractor, verify that the license is current and that it covers the appropriate trade. Also, check on complaints filed against the license. This information is available from your state's Contractor Board.

- **Define what you want and what you expect** from contractors and labor. Ask questions if you don't understand any aspect of the project.

- **Patience.** If you are remodeling during business hours, be prepared for the workers and the day's activities.

- **Build in incentives to ensure your job is a priority.** Yes, money talks. But so does a nice meal or a treat to take home to the family. This works great for everyone - from the owner to the clean-up crew.

- **Improve your communications with regular meetings.** Be available during crucial aspects of a project.

- **Hire the best and let them do their job.** Micromanaging the crew can backfire and create a hostile work environment.

Licenses, Bonds and Insurance

Part of the selection process for consultants, design firms and construction tradespeople is the review of licenses, bonds and insurance. All construction projects have some inherent risks, but reviewing these critical areas will, hopefully, protect you from potential liability and give you peace of mind. Consider the following:

- **Licenses are required of all businesses** (city, county and/or state). In addition, some trades and professions must also be licensed by your state (e.g., contractors, architects, interior designers, landscape architects, real estate brokers, land surveyors and engineers). Verify that all licenses are valid and current.

- **Construction bonds protect you against substandard work or code violations.** However, they offer no guarantee of financial stability or competency. Consult an attorney about whether your project warrants:
  - **Performance Bonds** that guarantee satisfactory completion of a project.
  - **Payment Bonds** that protect against liens for unpaid materials or labor.
  - **Contract Bonds** that combine the benefits of Performance and Payment Bonds.

- **Insurance coverage.** This should include workers' compensation, property damage and liability coverage. As the project owner, you can be held responsible for job-site injuries, property damage and other liabilities if your contractor is not adequately covered.

- **Verify.** Make sure that your service providers are appropriately licensed, adequately insured and have ample bond coverage:

- **Contact your Contractors Board** to verify your state's General and Specialty Contractors license, bonds and insurance requirements.

- **A helpful Web site is www.contractors-license.org,** where you can find your state's requirements and licensing board information.

- **Ask other professionals (architects, designers, consultants) for their trade certification** or a copy of their licenses.

- **Additional bond coverage would typically be required, as state requirements are often inadequate.** Ask your lawyer about what would be ample coverage.

- **Ask to see a copy of the certificate of insurance,** or ask for the name of the contractor's insurance carrier and agency to verify that the contractor has adequate insurance for the project.

- **Visit PeopleFind.com** at www.peoplefind.com/flip/professional_licenses.html. They verify professional licenses for a small fee.

CHAPTER THREE

CONSTRUCTION & RENOVATION

Selecting the Perfect Site

Selecting land for custom ground-up construction, "build to suit" locations and leased space is a complex decision. It's a blend of technical issues (e.g., flooding potential), market research (e.g., too many competitors), financial requirements (e.g., costly excavation) and governmental restrictions (e.g., liquor licensing). Also, consider the following issues:

• **Feasibility study.** If your budget can handle a feasibility study (figure $5,000 or more), experienced analysts can help take the guesswork out of the process. However, this can be cost prohibitive for many small-restaurant owners. Ask your other consultants and construction professionals to share their concerns and advice.

Tips and warning signals when selecting bare land, "build to suit" and leased space:

• **Associate yourself with an experienced commercial real estate broker.**

• **Obtain free site selection resources** and "Location Strategies" newsletter at www.locationstrategies.com.

• **Find a location with the appropriate zoning.** Unless you enjoy a battle, walk away from locations that require variances.

- **Check on the land's history.** Is the land a reclaimed dump site or marsh? Are mosquitoes or flies a problem in the area? Was it under water during the 100-year flood?

- **Determine if the elevation creates problems.** The view may be great, but will bad weather make the driveway impassable? Low elevations may create drainage and sewage problems. Are there accessibility issues for elderly or disabled customers?

- **Review the FEMA National Flood Insurance Web site** at: www.fema.gov/nfip. Every area of the country has been carefully mapped out for potential flooding and national flood insurance eligibility.

- **Select a well-shaped lot.** Is there ample room for parking? Can delivery and garbage trucks get to your back door? Is the frontage sufficient to be seen by potential customers driving by?

- **Beware of short-term leases.** You may prefer a shorter commitment, but you could be putting your restaurant in jeopardy and be forced to move or pay escalated rent.

- **Look at the traffic.** Will customers cross busy traffic lanes? Is there direct access? Are there freeway off-ramps or will the world pass you by at 65 miles per hour?

- **Verify that utilities are available and adequate for a busy restaurant** before you put down any money! Your commercial real estate broker and local utility companies can verify this.

- **Read** the "Location, Location, Location" section for more information.

Building Permits and Codes

Most construction and remodeling projects will require several different permits. These permits and subsequent inspections are to assure the public that your facility complies with the community's accepted standards for personal and environmental health and safety. Your architect, restaurant consultant and contractor should be diligent in their code compliance. Lack of attention can cost you time and money. Below are tips on handling permit and code issues that a typical restaurant will encounter:

- **Zoning.** Whether you purchase land or lease a building, your location must be zoned for your food service activities, including liquor licenses, music venues, retail sales and "after-hours" operations. Zone regulations will also affect signs, awnings, outdoor dining, parking and noise levels. Exceptions can be made, but it is best to find the location that most closely meets your needs without variances.

- **Covenants and restrictions.** Neighborhoods, malls and building complexes all may have covenants and restrictions that govern your business activities. Your real estate broker can assist you with these during lease or purchasing negotiations. Don't forget to inform your project manager and design team of these regulations.

- **Franchisee or licensee requirements.** Franchises and licensed concept companies are exacting in their requirements - many of which directly affect your construction and design efforts.

- **Building codes.** Your local building codes are adopted to protect the public. Compliance is mandatory and can sometimes be subjective, based upon an inspector's experience. Building codes control your design, construction methods and materials used. Equipment and fixtures, such as exhaust systems, ventilation, lighting and sanitation equipment, are all areas that must be "code approved."

- **Plumbing, mechanical and electrical codes.** These specific construction industries are generally overseen by separate permit requirements and inspection procedures.

- **Health department regulations.** No other public service department so directly impacts your food service business. Complex (and occasionally arcane) rules and regulations require diligent attention. This is a prime reason why your architects, consultants and contractors should have extensive local experience in restaurant development.

- **Americans with Disabilities Act.** The ADA defines accessibility and traffic-pattern requirements for people with disabilities. Most public facilities must meet these regulations.

Transforming Buildings into Restaurants

Over the past several decades, restaurateurs have been busily transforming warehouses, historical buildings, classic homes and churches, antique train stations, defunct banks, abandoned gas stations and old theaters into dining establishments. Economic declines, corporate mergers and neighborhood shifts have created an ample supply of vacant buildings, one of which, with some imagination and resources, can become the restaurant of your dreams. The functional requirements of preparing and serving food have their own set of challenges and, when coupled with converting untraditional locations, may present you with significant renovation costs. However, the rewards can be more than worth the effort and cost. If you haven't considered renovating an untraditional building, you might ponder some of the following and suggestions:

- **Consider bank buildings.** Mergers and acquisitions have created hundreds of vacant bank and savings-and-loans branches with great locations and plenty of parking.

- **Need a drive-up window?** Gas stations typically have ample space for window service and parking.

- **Renovating abandoned property.** This can be time consuming and costly. So why do it?
  - Love of a community.
  - Respect for the architecture and craftsmanship.
  - Access to antique hardware, stained glass, hardwood floors, hand-hewn cabinetry and other irreplaceable building materials.
  - Location in an overdeveloped area. Vacant lots can be hard to find, especially in the most actively developed neighborhoods.

- **Research government-backed reclamation projects.** Downtown redevelopment programs can underwrite a portion of your renovation costs, offer low-cost loans and provide you with great marketing resources. Grants may also be available in areas designated as economic-stimulus areas.

- **Contact state and private historical organizations, civic groups and preservation societies.** Learn about redevelopment districts and properties suitable for preservation.

- **Create a coalition of business owners.** Pool resources for revitalizing a building or city block.

- **Ask about financial incentives for converting underutilized buildings.** These can be license and permit waivers, tax abatements and financing subsidies.

New Construction Timeline

You've been dreaming for a lifetime about opening your own restaurant. Of course, once you've committed yourself, you want it to open now! So just how long will it take from concept through construction to your grand opening? New construction timelines are filled with pitfalls and unforeseen obstacles, and sometimes things even come in under schedule. A typical new construction project will take two years or more. Concept development, market research and financing can take a year. Acquiring land, licenses, architectural plans and blueprints will take another 8-10 months. The contractor bidding process can eat up 2-4 months. Restaurant equipment can take 6-8 weeks for delivery. Custom furniture may be backlogged for 8-12 weeks. You'll also need to plan for construction delays due to lack of materials and laborers. Here are some guidelines to help your project stay on track:

- **Be thorough when completing paperwork.** Loan documents, zoning variances, permits and licenses must be fully completed and accurate. When in doubt, ask before submitting. Government agencies aren't typically prepared to expedite resubmitted paperwork.

- **Introduce yourself to your future neighbors when zoning issues are a concern.** Meet with key businesses, residents and influential parties to build support. Gather supporters at public zoning meetings.

- **Use contractors and suppliers with reputations for timeliness.** Include completion-bonus clauses in contracts. Select a project team leader. Meet regularly.

- **Create a project management system.** Purchase an oversized expanding briefcase-style folder to keep important documents, notes and follow-up schedules. Keep this close to answer questions and locate information quickly.

- **Plan ahead.** Don't rush to start construction. Poor planning creates inevitable changes that delay schedules. These changes are rarely competitively bid (remember you've got people waiting) and can quickly escalate your project costs.

- **Empower people to make decisions.** Set parameters on decisions that your team members can make. Establish responsibilities and let people know whom they can go to for an answer.

Open for Business During a Renovation

Should you close the doors to remodel or hope that the customers don't notice the sawdust in the soup? Deciding whether or not to keep the doors open during a major renovation can be complicated. As a restaurateur, you must evaluate the immediate financial impact of empty seats and weigh the long-term effects of a closure. In some highly competitive markets, closing for even a few weeks could translate into an unrecoverable or costly decline in business. The following suggestions will help you weigh the pros and cons and cope with the process:

- **Speak with your contractor about your concerns.** Whenever possible, review and adapt the work schedule to your slow periods. "After-hours" or tight scheduling may cost more, but compare that to potential lost revenue.

- **Have your contractor detail the construction methods** to understand just how dusty, dirty, smelly or noisy your restaurant will be. A less-disruptive alternative method may be available. Compare cost versus convenience factors.

- **Establish a contract with stiff penalties for not meeting deadlines** to keep inconvenience and/or closure dates to a minimum.

- **Compute the cost of being closed for X number of days** and weigh that against the project requirements, reduced payroll costs, minimized inconvenience and potential customer exodus.

- **Cleaning up.** Write into your contract that all subcontractors and laborers will be responsible for daily cleanup, trash hauling and removal/disposal of all old materials and equipment.

- **Trust the experts.** Seek the advice and support of your contractor, designer, architect and restaurant consultant. They should be able to offer some creative solutions based on their direct experience.

- **Understand the situation and make the most of it.** Some renovations simply cannot be done in your spare time; they require 100 percent of your facility and pocketbook. Develop a "Closed for a New Look" plan to announce your closure and reopening. Take active steps to not be forgotten by your regulars and the community.

- **Close your restaurant during activities involving hazardous or "irritating" materials,** such as fiberglass insulation, lead paint or asbestos removal and pest-control procedures.

Working in a Construction Zone

Many redecorating and some renovation projects can be handled without a temporary closure. With some good communication and careful planning, your customers can be given a sneak preview of what's to come without being too inconvenienced. Here are some helpful hints:

Let customers and employees know what great things are happening.

- **Post regular updates for employees** along with some "sales talk" to help them speak with customers about the hammering in back!

- **Attach a personal note to your menu** thanking customers for their patience during construction.

- **Post humorous "Work in Progress" signs** and photos at the door or a display with architectural renderings.

- **Pass out "Re-Grand Opening" coupons** and celebratory invitations.

- **If wait times are extended, have a mini cocktail party in your waiting area.** Pass out wine samples, simple appetizers or freshly baked cookies. Use custom-printed napkins announcing your upcoming reopening celebration.

- **Avoid "smelly" activities during meal times.** Painting and sewer renovations are best handled during periods where customers are sparse.

- **Consider eliminating just one meal service.** Calculate your least profitable hours and schedule work then. Don't forget to clearly post your "new" hours in advance.

- **Break the project down by area as opposed to task.** Instead of paneling the entire dining room at lunchtime, speak with your renovation team about dividing the project area into smaller areas. This will probably increase your overall project cost, but customers will still be able to dine with minimal disturbance.

- **Route customers away from work areas.** Alter traffic patterns with freestanding signs, paintings on easels or decorative ropes. Rent these from party/catering-supply houses.

- **Police the work area throughout the day for potential safety issues.** Never put your staff or customers at risk.

- **Seal off work areas with heavyweight plastic sheeting.** Dust and debris are minimized and work areas less distracting.

- **Rent whole-room fans.** Draw dust and orders away from diners.

Creating Environments That Work with People

Ergonomics is the physical interaction of humans with spaces and objects during activities. A prep area that requires workers to stretch repeatedly across to reach ingredients and a broiler unit that only very tall workers can safely use are examples of "poor" ergonomics. Proper ergonomics in a restaurant can positively affect your employees' physical well-being, productivity and attitude. Ergonomically correct seating can also enhance your diners' experience. Here are some valuable tips to help you "engineer" your restaurant to work well with people. Additional in-depth information can be found in sections covering specific issues such as lighting, equipment, workflow and traffic patterns.

- **Temporary workstations.** Create mini work stations where all necessary food, utensils and prep space are close at hand.

- **Streamline.** Eliminate excessive bending, lifting and reaching while encouraging proper prep and storage procedures.

- **Seating.** Provide stools or chairs to give backs and feet a rest if the work being done doesn't require standing.

- **Make certain your tools and equipment weren't designed only for men.** Although more and more women are donning toques, tools and equipment haven't necessarily been redesigned to accommodate their shorter frames, smaller hands or other physical characteristics.

- **Ladders.** Provide stable, heavy-duty work ladders for accessing top shelves and deep storage units.

- **Left-handed staff.** Purchase a supply of important tools and utensils for left-handed employees.

- **Avoid congestion.** Arrange seating to minimize steps and reduce cross-traffic patterns.

- **Clientele comfort.** Make a point of minimizing your guests' exposure to glare, drafts and noisy areas.

- **Access.** Create easy entrances and exits.

- **Interaction.** Think about how employees, customers and vendors will interact with your facility. Do the physical environment, fixtures and equipment make it easier or more difficult to do a job or enjoy a meal?

- **Movable fixtures.** Choose fixtures and equipment that can be easily moved when needed.

Will You Have Enough Dining Space?

Space is frequently at a premium in public areas. So just how much space should you allow for eating, serving and other activities? What works in a crowded coffee shop won't meet the expectations of an elegant dinner house. Understanding your customers' expectations and their needs will help you to allocate your precious space. The following are some useful guidelines and tips that can be used to determine dining room layout and spacing:

- **Factor in your customers' needs.** Young people can tolerate being placed close together, while less mobile, older patrons may have walkers and canes to deal with.

- **Mixing up your table sizes and seating types can help** you direct traffic patterns through a room.

- **Consider using round tables,** which can accommodate more people and allow for easier access. However, they can be harder to place in a room and cannot be used along walls.

- **Check out the views from every table.** Try to avoid work stations, bathrooms, halls and other less-than-attractive sights.

- **Build in flexibility.** You need to be able to handle crowds and small parties.

- **Set aside sufficient work areas within the dining room.** See chapter 6, "Front-of-the-House Support Stations" for more information.

- **Wheelchair access.** Allow at least 32 inches of aisle space and a table height of 27-inches high by 30-inches wide by 19-inches deep.

Recommended standard spacing allowances:
- At least 18 inches between backs of chairs to avoid chair bumping and for servers and guests to pass.
- At least 24 inches for service aisles. Thirty-six inches is optimum.
- At least 48 inches for main aisles.
- At least 18 inches from the chair back to the table edge.
- About 12 inches from the seat cushion to the underside of the table for leg room.

Recommended dining room space allowance per seat:

Service Type	Square Feet Required per Seat
Banquet (minimum)	10 to 11
Buffet	12 to 18
Family Style	13 to 16
Fast Food	10 to 14
Tableside (minimum)	11 to 14
Tableside (upscale)	15 to 18
Counter	18 to 20

Traffic and Workflow

A well-designed restaurant makes it faster and easier to serve meals. Improper workflow and poor traffic patterns mean thousands of wasted steps and movements every day. Analyzing your layout and equipment needs from the viewpoint of the user will increase productivity, decrease employee stress and injuries and improve your customer service. Here are some areas of traffic within your restaurant and how you might eliminate excess steps and waiting, while increasing productivity:

- **Restrooms.** Place restrooms at the front of the restaurant to minimize traffic around the kitchen.

- **Hire a traffic/workflow expert.** A food service consultant specializing in traffic analysis and workflow streamlining can help you maximize your space while improving employee productivity.

- **Listen to your staff.** Service personnel, chefs and assistants with hands-on experience can help you create layouts that won't tire them, will help them to respond quicker and will improve morale.

- **Counter service.** Compare customer feelings on waiting versus service processes. With single lines, counter people typically handle specific tasks: order taking, assembly or cash handling. Multiple line service requires more registers, and each server handles all responsibilities. A single winding line is perceived to be a longer wait; however, throughput (actual customers served) is almost equal. Both line styles have similar space requirements.

- **Self-service/cafeteria location.** Centrally locate salad/dessert bars and cafeteria lines with ample walk space on all four sides whenever possible. Duplicate offerings on each side to minimize reaching and maximize the number of customers served per hour.

- **Maneuverability.** Estimate counter width at 14 feet: 4 feet for a customer aisle, 1 foot for a tray slide, 2 feet for counter width, 4.5 feet for counter workers and 2.5 feet for back bar. Make sure that trays, bins and service carts can fit between aisles and counter sides.

- **Use a single counter for the simplest customer traffic pattern.** Physical barriers can be used to create a directional flow and eliminate line disruption. Position food stations to minimize cross-traffic:
  - Desserts should be placed first in self-service venues if these are not included in all-you-can-eat pricing.
  - Hot items and made-to-order foods should be positioned just prior to the beverages.
  - Drinks should be the last food item before cashiers and/or seating to avoid potential spills.

More Workflow Advice

Seeing where every table and workstation is placed in relationship to each other, how they relate to the active prep areas and the kitchen, will help you to eliminate unnecessary steps, cross-traffic and backtracking. Consider the following:

- **Table service.** Diagram the room. Some design engineers can create helpful 3-D illustrations detailing the number of steps between tables and work areas.

- **Party areas.** Place banquet and large party areas closest to the kitchen to improve service and food delivery times.

Review outside access to and serviceability of exterior dining areas:
- Eliminate stepping down through a doorway.
- Include a fully stocked work area to avoid extra trips inside.

Enhance communication to reduce steps and speed service:
- Centrally located or multiple-station POS equipment. Even more efficient, handheld order-entry systems allow the waitstaff to move directly to the next customer.
- Vibrating pagers and two-way radios to signal that tables are cleared or meals are ready.

Back-of-the-House

Too many people, too little space, too much work to get done in too short a time! Sounds like a busy restaurant. Good traffic patterns and workflow make it easier for your chef and support staff to be productive. Consider the following:

- **Add traffic aisles.** Thirty inches is the minimum to allow traffic to move around the kitchen without interfering with active workspace. Be certain that aisles are wide enough for mobile carts. Heavy-traffic areas or aisles with workers on each side may require 48 inches or more.

- **Access.** Add extra doors for direct bar access.

- **Streamline procedures.** Implement a straight-line workflow for products such as sandwiches.

- **Maximize workspace.** Place single-purpose equipment next to the active workspace and shared equipment between two work centers.

Install separated kitchen access doors:
- Separate doors should be 2 feet apart.
- Doors should only swing one way with large, clear, unbreakable windows in each.
- Clearly mark doors - IN or OUT - on each side.
- Doors should be at least 42-inches wide.
- If separate doors aren't possible, use double-swinging doors (at least 84-inches).

CHAPTER FOUR

ENVIRONMENTAL & SAFETY ISSUES

General Issues

From proper waste-water systems to scrubbable materials, environmental and safety concerns are essential to good restaurant design. With careful planning, you can create a building that promotes cleanliness and safety. Failing to address these issues properly can put your customers, employees and business at risk.

- **Review.** During the planning stage, carefully review all design and purchasing decisions to ensure your restaurant:
  - Complies with local building and sanitation codes.
  - Minimizes exposure to lawsuits from customer injuries and food-related illnesses.
  - Protects employees from injuries that result in lost productivity and escalating workers' compensation costs.
  - Creates a clean and inviting environment for customers.

- **When making construction and design choices,** don't forget:
  - Suitable work areas that prevent cross-contamination situations.
  - Ample storage for good food-handling procedures and to eliminate cluttered floors.
  - Cleanable materials must hold up to scrubbing, steam/hot water and chemical agents.

- Ample lighting in common areas, workstations and "danger zones" to minimize accidents.
- Proper drainage in wet areas (prep, restrooms) to prevent slip-and-fall injuries.
- Appropriate nonslip or slip-resistant flooring material for high-traffic and wet areas.

Real and Perceived Cleanliness Issues

Visible and perceived sanitation issues should be of paramount concern for every restaurateur. Customer sophistication and media attention of food-borne illnesses have fueled food-safety concerns. The cleanliness of your public areas is a direct reflection of your concern for sanitation behind closed doors.

- **Pay close attention to kitchen and work areas visible** from the dining area. The natural chaos of a busy restaurant can give the impression that food may not be safely prepared.

- **Give the customer assurance that no unseen germs are lurking.** Your restaurant shouldn't just appear clean and tidy; it should have no undesirable smells, no wobbly chairs and no dirty air vents.

- **Don't skimp on the restroom fixtures.** No matter what your budget, special attention should be paid to the restrooms. Customers prefer restrooms where contact with surfaces is minimized, towels are plentiful, waste is contained, water isn't wasted and babies can be diapered and fed.

The Air We Breathe

Healthy air, inside and out, is a business and moral concern that impacts restaurants legally and financially. Poor air quality contributes directly to employee absenteeism and unhappy customers. Many communities have rigid air-emission and work-environment regulations relating to proper ventilation, wood burning, grease and smoke. Unpleasant odors also contribute to poor air quality. Bear in mind the following:

- **Indoor air.** Wood-burning ovens, charbroilers, fryers and "sealed" buildings can all create unhealthy or unpleasant air conditions. Indoor air quality requires bringing sufficient outdoor air in, properly filtering recirculated air and directing airflow.

- **Smoking.** In addition, cigar and/or cigarette smoking issues are highly debated within the hospitality industry. Local and state regulations vary widely across the U.S. Your state chapter of the National Restaurant Association can keep you apprised on current and pending regulations.

Helpful tips on improving indoor air quality:
- **Physically separate smoking and non-smoking dining areas** and/or direct airflow away from non-smoking tables. Ban employee smoking in the kitchen, dining room and bar.

- **Install a whole-building air cleaner/filtration system** that also reduces airborne particles and dust.

- **Check for radon, mold spores and biological dangers** when converting older or long-vacant buildings.

- **Incorporate plants** such as peace lilies, dracaena and English ivy to help naturally clean the air. Read *How to Grow Fresh Air: 50 Houseplants to Purify Your Home or Office* by B.C. Wolverton (Penguin USA).

- **See what the EPA says about indoor air quality** at www.epa.gov/iaq/pubs/insidest.html.

- **Be aware of unhealthy emissions** from carpeting, paint and cleaning products. Sick Building Syndrome is explained at the National Safety Council site at www.nsc.org/ehc/indoor/sbs.htm.

- **Visit the Phillip Morris USA Web site.** Options, www.pmoptions.com, is dedicated to indoor air quality issues. You'll also find free assessment tools and an HVAC (heating, ventilation and air-conditioning) referral service.

- **Hire an HVAC contractor or engineer with restaurant experience.** HVAC contractors install new systems or maintain existing systems, while an HVAC engineer designs and specifies systems.

- **Join the Hospitality Coalition on Indoor Air Quality** at www.hciaq.org.

Outdoor Air Quality Issues

Imagine the tantalizing aroma from a wood-burning pizza oven, a melt-in-your-mouth doughnut and the richer taste of a charbroiled burger. Fireplaces, wood-burning ovens, fryers, charbroilers and other cooking equipment all emit particulates - gases, grease and odors - that are regulated by local, state and federal environmental standards. Local and state standards vary greatly and, in some instances, the Federal Air Quality standards may supersede these. Close attention should be paid to these regulations, as penalties can be severe. Here are some helpful ideas on how to comply with emission regulations:

- **Air filters.** Hire an industrial air-cleaning firm to install emission-control systems that handle grease, smoke, carbon dioxide and odors.

- **Vents/ducts.** Inspect and repair all exterior vents, hoods and intake ducts on existing or older equipment. Maintenance not only saves the air, it also saves you in energy costs. Dirty, inadequate or old systems are big electricity wasters.

- **Humidity.** Purchase wood for ovens or fireplaces with 20 percent or less of moisture if you use a decorative wood-burning fireplace or wood-fired oven. This means drying times of 6-8 months. Store wood with a clear polyethylene drape to promote drying. Keep sides open for circulation.

- **Review the report on proper wood oven ventilation** by Vent Master at www.ventmaster.com/stainlessreports/srpdfs/sr52.pdf.

- **Install a catalytic oxider** that converts gases and smoke to water. For more information, read the Products Finishing Magazine article at www.pfonline.com/articles/010203.html.

- **Further information**. Contact your natural gas and electric utility companies, along with your county or state Environmental or Health Department for air-quality information, resources and financial incentives. The Southern California Air Quality Management District, with some the most stringent air quality regulations in the nation, offers comprehensive information at www.aqmd.gov.

- **Hire an air quality consultant.** He or she can to assist you with more complex emission issues and stringent regulations.

Water, Water, Everywhere and Not a Drop to Drink

In some communities, a glass of water isn't very appetizing. Unsavory odors and harsh tastes, along with hard-water deposits, are common issues. Unseen bacteria and pollutants may also be a concern. Poor water can adversely affect your food quality, damage equipment and tableware and disturb health-conscious diners. If a floating lemon slice isn't enough, a water "cleaning" system may be your best bet.

Filtration systems act like a very fine sieve. Filters also attract and hold even smaller particles and dissolved molecules. Filters are rated by the particle size they remove. The smallest bacteria are one-half micron while visible "dirt" ranges up from 40 microns. Activated carbon is a common filter medium. Invest in the best filtration system your establishment can afford. Here are some tips on offering your customers clean, fresh and tasty water:

- **Determine what's in your water.** Your water department or independent testing company can provide a profile of your water's composition (solids, hardness, chlorine levels). Select equipment that addresses your water's "bad" elements. Besides safe and tasty water, your specific chemical and equipment needs for washing produce, equipment and dishware are affected by your water's composition.

- **"Undercounter" systems.** If whole "house" systems aren't a cost-effective choice, incorporate smaller, undercounter models to provide clean water for prep sinks, beverage makers/dispensers and cooking-water faucets.

- **Easy cleaning.** Look for filtration systems that can be cleaned easily or use inexpensive replaceable filters. Filters should be ample enough for a 6-month maintenance cycle.

- **Ice makers.** Don't overlook clean, filtered water for ice makers.

- **Chlorine reduction.** Choose systems that can reduce chlorine levels to approximately .5 parts per million for the best tasting coffee and tea.

- **Serve high-profit sparkling and destilled bottled water.** Some customers prefer the "safety" of bottled water opened at the table with a flourish!

Conserving Energy

Restaurant environmental systems and equipment require an enormous amount of energy. The National Restaurant Association reports potential profit increases at 4-4.5 percent of revenue, simply by reducing energy consumption by 25 percent.

Energy-conscious construction methods, along with energy-efficient equipment and environmental systems, are wise investments. Although initial costs may be greater, your ROI could actually offset the full cost of the equipment over its life span. Here are some tips to help you create an energy-wise restaurant:

- **Free energy assessment.** Have your local utility company complete a free energy assessment on your existing restaurant. They can monitor the efficiency of your walk-in freezer, cooler or fryer to help you determine your actual energy cost per month for each. Use these figures to compute potential energy savings if you replaced the unit with a more efficient model.

- **Concentrate first on the major energy users.** HVAC systems account for 30-50 percent of your annual electricity costs. A sit-down restaurant can figure annual costs at about $1.10 per square foot for heating, cooling and ventilation.

- **Don't overlook small ways to make savings.** For example, use more efficient light bulbs, programmable thermostats and plastic strips on walk-in refrigerators.

- **Investigate the EPA's Energy Star program.** It's designed to help small businesses become more energy efficient. Visit www.epa.gov/smallbiz for restaurant-specific information.

- **Watch for the Energy Star label on products** from lamps to commercial freezers. Review manufacturers' energy consumption data and anticipated equipment life.

- **Improvements**. Seek out private and government lenders who specialize in financing energy-related improvements for the most favorable interest rates.

- **Financial incentives.** Contact your utility companies about subsidies, rebates and financial incentives for replacing inefficient equipment with approved models. Your tax accountant can also advise you on state or federal tax incentives.

- **Hire an energy consultant.** Ask him or her to make recommendations on your design and equipment choices.

- **Invest in your bottom line with long-term payoffs for your restaurant and our environment.** Energy costs have historically risen, so your savings factor could be even more significant in future years.

Waste Management

Handling food, oil, grease and solid waste takes time, effort and money. Waste management and reduction are not only cost-effective, they are wise environmental and business choices. Your efforts can actually become a marketing advantage. Customers really do appreciate knowing that their favorite restaurant cares enough to reduce, recycle and properly dispose of waste. Here are some helpful ideas on managing and reducing your restaurant waste and disposal costs:

- **Check on local waste management requirements early** in the project. Municipal standards vary widely. Some jurisdictions may require retrofitting existing buildings when ownership changes.

- **Install a properly sized commercial grease trap** and/or interceptor. The Plumbing and Drainage Institute at 800-589-8956 or www.pdionline.org has comprehensive articles and member referral information. Grease containment equipment can run to as much as $20,000 to install.

- **Research bioaugmentation.** Biological elements "digest" the fat and grease, reducing the amount of waste your system must handle. Visit the Wastewater Bioaugmentation Resource Web site at www.bioaugmentation.com for more information.

- **Research local providers.** This is real science, but "quacks" are common. Check references carefully.

- **Purchase a waste disposal unit.** Look for stainless steel units with automatic reversal controls. Select units with ample horsepower and rotor size to handle your typical food waste. Invest in long-term performance when comparison-shopping.

- **Build a recycling center and establish a usage program.** Include recycling equipment in your back-of-the-house layout. Contact grease/meat waste rendering companies about pickup. A directory is available from Rendering Magazine at www.rendermagazine.com/pages/NRA2001Directory.pdf. Make it easy for employees to comply by incorporating sorting bins and conveniently located waste receptacles. Install color-coded recycling containers on wheels.

- **Cardboard balers.** Be prepared to handle large quantities of paper, cardboard, plastics, glass, metal cans and food waste. Cardboard balers can pay for themselves through reduced hauling costs.

- **Invest in a commercial-grade trash compactor.** Even with the most aggressive recycling program, you still will have trash. A compactor will pay for itself quickly by maximizing bin use and hauling fees.

It's Good to Be Green

As Kermit the Frog knows - it's good to be green. In this case, we are speaking of environmentally friendly "green" building products and construction methods. This growing segment within the construction trades focuses on products and techniques that promote health, safety, energy conservation, waste management and recycling.

Businesses of all sizes are discovering the financial, personal and community benefits of "being green." Here are some resources for learning more about creating a less wasteful and more ecologically productive business:

- **Learn more about the green construction movement** and how it can improve your bottom line at:
  - Green Architect at www.archrecord.com/GREEN/GREEN.ASP.
  - U.S. Department of Energy at www.eren.doe.gov/buildings/commercial_roadmap.

- **Look for grants, low-interest loans and funding** for green construction:
  - Funding Green Buildings (www.fundinggreen-

buildings.com) is funding consultants specializing in green building.

- ShoreBank Pacific offers eco-loans for Pacific Northwest businesses. Visit www.eco-bank.com.
- Fat Earth at www.fatearth.com offers a financing resource directory and other information on paying for energy saving and green construction and equipment.

- **Hire green building professionals.** A service directory can be found at Greenbuilder.com at www.greenbuilder.com or by searching Yahoo's Business Directory by the keyword "green building."

- **Pick up a book on the subject.** As this is a rapidly changing industry, select the newest books available. Popular titles include:
  - *Green Building Handbook: A Companion Guide to Building Products and Their Impact on the Environment* by Tom Wolley.
  - *Green Building Materials: A Guide to Product Selection and Specification* by Ross Spiegel and Dru Meadows.

- **Require your architect and builder to comply with the EPA's Energy Star Design Target program.** Details at http://yosemite1.epa.gov/estar/business.nsf/content/nbd_targetfinder.htm#1.

- **Research sustainable and green resources** at Fat Earth at www.fatearth.com. Search for restaurant-specific information using the keyword "restaurant."

- **Use your green-building efforts as a springboard** for free local and regional publicity.

- **Register your building and efforts** with the EPA's Energy Star program.

Heating, air Conditioning and ventilation are vital for your restaurant.

CHAPTER FIVE

BUILDING SYSTEMS

Warm in the Winter and Cool in the Summer

Maintaining comfortable, ambient temperatures is difficult in a food service environment where heat-producing equipment battles with cooling and heating systems. The challenge is to create an environment where fast-moving workers won't collapse from heat exhaustion and relaxing diners don't shiver - all without bankrupting your operational budget. Consider the following suggestions to help you master your heating, ventilation and air-conditioning (known collectively as HVAC):

- **Invest in the most energy-efficient unit** you can afford. Up to 50 percent of your total energy use is for HVAC systems. Even a modest reduction means significant operational savings.

- **Explore remote monitoring and energy assessment** services. Read about Applebee's success with Pentech Solutions (www.pentechsd.com).

- **Combat mold/spore growth and humidity** with proper ventilation systems. Restaurant kitchens are often overly humid, contributing to faster spoilage and potential health problems. Visit The Hospitality Coalition on Indoor Air Quality at www.hciaq.org/index.htm for more information.

- **Air filters.** Make certain your filters have at least a 65-percent dust spot efficiency rating to reduce airborne particulates.

- **Consider installing heat-control window glazing** to reduce dining room temperatures. Called low-e coating, this high-tech solution blocks heat-producing rays without reducing the incoming light. To learn more, visit Efficient Windows at www.efficientwindows.org.

- **Include heat-absorbing materials** in your construction and design. These naturally absorb heat during the warmer hours and release it slowly at night.

- **Ask your HVAC consultant about heat recovery equipment.** This equipment redirects "wasted" heat (energy) that is normally vented to the outside and reuses it to heat dishwasher water and warm other spaces. Request a cost analysis report to determine potential savings.

- **Don't overlook updating HVAC equipment and systems** when doing any major overhaul. You can save as much as 50 percent in energy costs by replacing systems that are ten years or older. Utility company financing and grants may be available for these energy upgrades.

- **Minimize airflow noises.** Incorporate larger air ducts in dining areas and direct A/C vents in order to minimize excessive cooling of food waiting to be served.

Putting the Fire Out

Industry experts say more than 1,000 restaurant kitchen fires occur each day. Protecting property from fire and smoke means using suitable fire-resistant and retardant materials, installing detectors and properly maintaining suppression systems. Your sprinkler system can be a real lifesaver. Commercial fire-suppression systems are networks of piping that sprinkle water or chemicals to douse fires. Handheld extinguishers are your first line of defense in a fire. Here are some practical fire-prevention tips:

- **Hire only licensed installers.** Many states require special licensing for contractors and installers of fire suppression equipment.

- **Update any system installed prior to 1994.** The Underwriters Laboratory updated UL-300 standards in November 1994. Equipment changes and the switch from lard to vegetable-based oils, which create "hotter" and more difficult-to-manage fires, make older equipment inadequate in battling modern-day kitchen fires.

- **Purchase commercial fire extinguishers** designed specifically for restaurant kitchens. These extinguishers use extinguishing agents suitable for typical commercial kitchen fires. Choose an appropriate size for the fire-producing capability of the specific work area. Train all staff members on proper operation of the units. Hire a firm to inspect and recharge units as required by your local fire department.

- **Install an automatic gas shut-off system** to reduce a fire's "food" - and the potential of explosions. Also, read the National Restaurant Association's booklet "Ensuring Fire Safety in Your Operation" for comprehensive fire-safety information. Call 800-765-2122, extension 70, and ask for publication MG523.

- **Make certain all construction and decorative materials meet or exceed fire and building codes:**
  - Select fireproof roofing and other fire-rated building products.
  - Ask your insurance agent about potential savings when using these materials.
  - It may be necessary to treat all drapery and fabrics with fire retardant.
  - Make certain that oven mitts, towels, uniforms, chef coats, hats and aprons are flame-resistant. No nylon, polyester, rayon or acetate-based fabrics should be used.

Hot and Cold Running Water

Sufficient hot and cold water are important resources in food preparation and service. Here are some things you should consider when heating, cooling, softening and using water:

- **Install water softeners** and use appropriate chemicals (detergents) to handle hard water. Hard water can clog pipes, create equipment malfunctions and spot (even damage) glassware, flatware and dishes.

- **Read about water quality issues** in chapter 4, "Environmental and Safety Issues."

- **Determine water availability and pressure before purchasing** or leasing property. Rural and desert communities aren't the only areas where potable water can be in short supply. Water pressure may seem unimportant, but insufficient pressure can affect dishwasher operation and cycle times, toilet flushing and automatic ice production.

- **Figure how much water you'll need per person served:**
  - 5 gallons or more for prep and drinking
  - 1.8 gallons for dishwashing by machine and slightly less by hand

- **Save on plumbing costs**. Place water heaters close to the equipment or sink to save heating dollars. This means you won't have to superheat (160° F) water to get 130° F at the tap. Insulate tanks and lines to minimize heat loss. Save plumbing costs by placing similar equipment and installations in groupings. Like needs can be placed side-by-side, back-to-back or, in multistory restaurants, above each other.

- **Consider booster heaters** as a cost-efficient way to maintain temperatures. Choose low-temp dishwashers or dishwashing equipment with built-in boosters.

- **Select water heaters with ample capacity** for your peak usage periods and quick recovery. Your food service consultant can help you calculate your needs.

- **Plan ahead.** For example, you may require special plumbing for items such as fish tanks, indoor plants and truck-washing areas.

Sounds Good to Us

The sound of the cash register ringing is wonderful! However, add that sound to clinking glasses, echoing conversations, swinging doors and clanging pots, and you've got a noisy restaurant. Eating and conversation go hand in hand, but unnecessary noise can spoil a dining experience. Excessive noise can also distress workers and increase fatigue. The object is not to create a sound vacuum but to minimize disturbing sounds while allowing conversations to be held at normal voice levels. You may even need to enhance sounds with background music or sound-reflecting materials. Here are some ways to help you create a positive sound environment:

- **Reduce or stop sound at the source.** Equipment located in or near public areas should operate as quietly as possible and be regularly maintained to minimize distracting noises.

- **Music.** To learn how to add music to your restaurant, read the section in the next chapter entitled "Music to Stimulate, Soothe and Woo."

- **Locate ice machines and other compressor-run equipment in the kitchen** whenever possible.

Use conveniently placed ice bins and other service containers in the front-of-the-house.

- **Save on energy costs.** Insulate windows, plumbing and HVAC ducts to dampened rushing sounds.

- **Add doors, decorative screens and glass partitions** to redirect sound away from dining areas. Be careful when using glass, as it actually amplifies some high-frequency sounds.

- **Use rubber mats throughout the kitchen.** They reduce direct and reflective sound and are more comfortable to walk on.

- **Consider carpeting, drapes and furniture as sound absorbers.** Generally, thicker materials provide better sound-deadening qualities.

- **Select only acoustical materials and treatments rated for restaurant use.** They should meet sanitation/cleaning standards, withstand moisture levels and have appropriate fire ratings.

- **Hire a sound expert** (acoustical consultant, sound engineer) who can assess your noise levels and recommend ways to incorporate sound-positive materials and sound-deadening efforts.

- **Introduce other ambient sounds** from strategically positioned fountains, muted background music or nature sounds (birds chirping, bubbling brooks) to mask undesirable noises.

Planning and Pre-wiring Specialty Systems

Planning ahead for your telephone, sound system, TV and cable, alarms, computer network and point-of-sale equipment is an important step in building or renovating your restaurant. Proper planning can save you money, establish the scheduling of the specialty contractor or service-provider and ensure that everyone is prepared when they arrive on-site. Here are some hints to help you plan and install specialty systems for today and tomorrow:

Review your immediate and potential future requirements:

- **Will the wiring need to be replaced** when you upgrade equipment or expand your system?

- **Will you need to tear out a wall to make a change?** A penny spent now can save hundreds later on.

- **Timescale.** Complete your equipment purchase, and schedule pre-wiring and wiring stages early, in order to avoid damaging fragile materials and finish work.

- **Phone lines.** Plan ahead for dedicated phone lines and electrical circuits along with convenient access to controls and outlets. Watch out for areas of your layout where changes may be made regularly and accommodate for shifting tables and rearranged décor.

- **Hide the wires!** Not only are exposed wires unsightly, they also can be potential safety hazards.

- **Hire a skilled consultant** specializing in the system you need. An independent expert can help you sort through technical issues, analyze a vendor's sales pitch and decipher the manufacturer's data.

- **Clarify who will be responsible for scheduling and reviewing a system installer's work.** Service-providers, like your local cable company, need to be supervised like any other subcontractor. Your design team leader, associated consultant or project manager can "supervise" these vendors, including keeping them informed of all pertinent changes, installation revisions and scheduling.

Think about a theme!

CHAPTER SIX

FRONT-OF-THE-HOUSE

The Universe of Theme Restaurants – Develop a Theme

What is a theme restaurant? A restaurant concept that defines, overwhelmingly, the brand instead of its good food and service? A restaurant that tantalizes all of the senses? A masterful blend of fun and fine dining? Thousands of different theme concepts have been launched over the years. Some became stale quickly; others thrived in spite of changing trends. Drawing boards across the U.S. are continuously filled with interesting ideas on combining entertainment and dining. Whether your theme restaurant is a solo project or major corporate effort, the same basic principles apply; a successful theme restaurant requires considerable capital, great marketing, impeccable timing, extensive research and an in-depth understanding of your market and target audience. Consider the following:

- **Look for theme concepts.** For example, investigate popular culture (e.g., video games, fashion, music and celebrities), "favorite memories" (e.g., a honeymoon in Paris, visiting Grandma's house or the prom), the unknown or unfamiliar (e.g., the Wild West, Victorian England or Atlantis) or hobbies (e.g., deep-sea fishing, golf or alpine skiing).

- **Focus on feelings, not just looks.** Tap into the nine basic human emotions - security, adventure, freedom, exchange, power, expansion, acceptance, community and express.

- **Read the Institute of Management Excellence's newsletter** on emotional needs at www.itstime.com/jun97.htm.

- **Target a specific audience.** Carefully review your ideal-customer profile to understand your audience's emotional needs and spending habits.

- **Do your homework.** Comprehensive marketing research and analysis is your verification to investors and partners that the profit potential makes it worth opening up the checkbook. Hire a consultant specializing in theme development.

- **Watch your timing.** Capturing the momentum of any trend is critical. Too soon or too late and you've failed.

Entertain ALL the senses:
- **Convince the ears.** Thunder and rain, hip-hop music, wild birds.
- **Delight the eyes.** Create a fantasy, recreate history, travel to another country.
- **Entice the nose.** Wildflower scents, fresh popcorn, banana-breath.
- **Encourage the fingers.** Elegant leather, furry mascots, touchable trinkets.
- **Tantalize the tongue.** Ethnic cuisine, comfort food, kiddy favorites.
- **Stimulate the mind.** Fascinate, delight, mystify.

- **Build upon the theme.** Every single physical and emotional element that the visitor encounters must add to the illusion. Every surface is a design opportunity. Ordinary items become artistic renderings. Your theme becomes the foundation for your brand.

- **Develop a network of creative talents** with multiple disciplines. Many theme restaurants require one-of-a-kind décor items. Even ordinary items like napkins may need an artist's reinterpretation.

- **Consider a design focal point concept instead.**
  Read the following section for information on a less
  entertainment-focused, more food-oriented approach.

Creating a Design Focal Point

Not every restaurant is a "theme" restaurant, but all
restaurants should have a theme. What we are
referring to is a design concept that accentuates your food
and is a starting point from which to develop your brand.
To avoid confusion with full-blown "theme" restaurants, let
us call this your "design focal point." Consider the
following:

- **Choose a design focal point that reflects your
  vision and build upon it.** For example, if your focus
  is apples, incorporate it in your:
  - **Restaurant name** - Apple Annie Café.
  - **Logo, signs** - bright red apple with green leaf.
  - **Uniforms** - red aprons, apple-shaped nametags.
  - **Decorative accents** - apple-red and white tile,
    apple-shaped cookie jars.
  - **Menus** - apple-shaped, apple photos or apple-
    related colors.
  - **Specialty items** - apple pie, apple bran muffins.
  - **Music** - Well, you get the idea!

- **Be subtle and keep gimmicks to a minimum.**
  Theme restaurants frequently emphasize entertainment over food. With your design focal point, you'll
  encourage customers to order meal enhancements
  (profitable drinks, appetizers and desserts), increase
  repeat business and develop your brand.

- **Avoid clichés and create an original look.** Theme
  restaurants embrace clichés and often overwork
  them. Your décor can be influenced, without being
  stereotypical, through familiar colors and subtle

elements. Blend the unique and unusual - as fusion cooking blends divergent flavors and styles.

- **Choose a design focal point that has no point at all.** Design for a feeling using multiple elements that make you think; elegant, cozy, warm, safe, wealthy, rested, young, indulgent.

- **Plan for the future.** Restaurant décor has a 5-7 year lifespan. Concentrate on versatile and neutral foundation elements (floors, lights, ceilings and fixtures) that won't need to be tossed when you redecorate.

- **Spend more on quality basics and save on the decorative touches.** Unlike restaurants where everything is part of the total look, using a design focal point allows you to accessorize without breaking the budget.

- **Don't "overdesign."** Use blank spaces (bare walls, neutral floors) to ease the eye. Resist the impulse to overwhelm the diner.

All in the Family

Creating a family-oriented restaurant requires more than handing out coloring books and providing high chairs. Kid-friendly environments are also environments that make it easier for parents to dine out. Appealing to the tykes is your primary goal (parents universally understand the power of pleasing them and keeping them quiet). However, your secondary goal is to enhance the dining experience for adults. Please both, and you'll ensure that parents and kids alike will want to return. Remember, the typical family unit is much different now. You now have weekend dads and moms, baby-boomer grandparents and second families blending adult and preschool siblings. Demographics show that today's parents and grandparents are more youth-oriented, active and willing to spend significant dollars on entertaining children. Eating out is an important part their daily lives, and the entertainment factor is a purchasing consideration - whether it is a take-out or sit-down affair.

- **Foster a fun atmosphere** with cheerful music (watch out for "Top 40" lyrics that might offend), bold colors and touchable surfaces.

- **Create seating areas that are sized to accommodate small children**, without squeezing adults. Surfaces within reach of toddlers and preschoolers should "hide" fingerprints and hold up to regular scrubbing.

- **Create a "family" restroom,** if space allows, where parents can take children to change diapers and nurse in safety and privacy.

- **Make certain there are ample stalls** that can accommodate a child and an attending adult.

- **Have a designated area for diaper changing in all restrooms.** A simple table or wall unit is better than placing baby on a wet counter or floor. Also, don't forget a supply of chemical wipes to sanitize surfaces. Place sinks, towel dispensers, dryers and waste receptacles within reach of small children. Provide a chair or designated area in the ladies' room for nursing mothers.

- **Eliminate "blind areas."** This enables parents to have a clear view of all exits, easily see their children enter and exit bathrooms and watch separate play areas.

- **Create a "kids welcome" area** in upscale restaurants. Parents will feel more comfortable and other diners won't be disturbed. Provide bike racks, along with interior and exterior stroller parking.

- **Use sound-absorbing materials** and enhance the acoustics to minimize ambient noise. Reduce harsh sounds to keep parents more relaxed.

The Night Life

Late-night restaurants, bars and lounges, nightclubs and after-hour joints share some specific needs and concerns. When handling night-life issues, from customer/employee safety to decorating dark environments, bear in mind the following:

- **Review your exterior for safety** and accessibility issues in the dark. Walk totally around the building and through the parking lot on a moonless night. Protecting patrons is good business and a legal necessity. Install automatic lighting with sensors. Trim shrubbery to eliminate "blind spots." Install handrails or fencing to direct people. Provide clear directional signage to doors and parking.

Create an interior designed for security:
- Face workstations, tills and cash registers towards the door.
- Incorporate a subtle, attractive element along all exits to help employees judge the height of a fleeing robber.
- Integrate security cameras into the décor. Check out smoke detectors that double as security cameras. Your security expert can advise you which cameras should be in full display as a deterrent.
- Build drop-safes into the floor.
- Place smashproof lights above all exterior doors and unbreakable windows in back doors.

- **Eliminate deep shadows and glaring lights** at entrances and exits. This makes it easier to see who's coming and going, minimizes eye-adjustment time and reduces potential slip-and-fall injuries.

- **Beef up insulation and sound deadening** capabilities. At night, even normal noise levels and ambient music can be disruptive to neighbors.

- **Incorporate more indirect lighting.** Light spaces, not people, to enhance the mood effectively.

- **Make evening dining outdoors more comfortable** with portable lighting and gas heaters. Watch for poorly-lit walk surfaces and doorways.

- **Use color liberally.** Just because the lights are down doesn't mean that colors cannot be seen. Gone are the days of black walls. Think bold burgundy or deep royal blue with metallic accents to catch the light.

- **Be prepared for smokers.** In communities that allow public smoking, invest in a state-of-the-art air-filtration system for customer and worker safety. Smoking rates increase during the late-night hours, especially in liquor-oriented venues.

- **Create a separate cigar-smoking lounge.** High-tech décor and trendy wines or overstuffed leather chairs and 25-year-old Port are two examples of catering to the upscale cigar aficionado.

Show Time - Display Kitchens

Dining as entertainment has taken on a new twist over the past decade. Food lovers enjoy watching the show. However, bringing the kitchen out front creates a vastly different work environment for the chef and staff. When designing a display kitchen emphasize the theatrics. Merchandise your food and make it the focal point of the room. Display kitchens require more expensive equipment. Ordinary galvanized and worn equipment won't cut it. "Design over function" requirements will significantly inflate your budget. Consider the following:

- Offset these expenses by minimizing other dining room décor.
- Create eye-catching counters and backdrops using decorative painting techniques, inexpensive mosaics or oversized tiles.
- Transform traditional stainless steel equipment into decorative elements by covering visible surfaces with tile, copper, brass or heat-resistant enamel paint.

- **Use easy-to-clean materials, worktables and layouts** that hide "clutter" and "dirt." An open kitchen must appear exceptionally clean, fresh and inviting. "Less attractive" prep should be handled behind closed doors.

- **Utilize lights to create drama** for the diner without sacrificing work needs.

- **Emphasize continual activity.** A display kitchen with little excitement is a waste. Incorporate open flames, intricate carving stations, sizzling woks and grills. Equipment should be placed so the chef faces the "audience."

- **Privacy.** Place equipment on bases or use "privacy" panels to hide unattractive legs, garbage and clutter.

- **Move specific tasks out front.** Transform preparing fresh tortillas, hand-kneading gourmet breads and creating elegant desserts into a show.

- **Quality.** Fill glass-front refrigeration units and display cases with fresh ice and attractive raw ingredients to send a message of quality and freshness.

- **Incorporate wood-burning-style (wood or gas) ovens with elegant stone hearths and brick interiors.** Copper, tile, stone and brick surrounds turn ovens into artistic statements.

- **Stimulate appetites with rotisseries.** These space-efficient sales tools can create succulent chickens, aromatic roasts and colorful casseroles in a 30-inch counter unit or a 6-foot floor-mounted display.

- **Don't skimp on your exhaust system.** Off odors and smoke clouds will quickly chase away diners!

The Best Seats in the House

The best seats in the house are now in full view of all the action. Special "chef's tables" or "kitchen tables" have become a trendy part of the fine-dining experience. Savvy food-lovers wait months for these coveted tables in Commander's Palace (New Orleans) or the Biltmore Hotel (Los Angeles). Even more casual chains such as Buca di Beppo (Minneapolis-based) have 50 units with highly profitable chef's tables. A National Restaurant Association 2000 industry study discovered four out of ten adults expressed an interest in display cooking - where food prep becomes entertainment. You can capture this audience by bringing a select few into the chef's domain. Bring your customers into your kitchen!

- **Safety.** Remember that diners need to be safely escorted and seated away from potential hazards. Check local health regulations regarding table placement. Some communities may require a low wall to separate the table from active work areas.

- **Create an entertaining, voyeuristic environment.** The heat, noise and chaos are part of the charm - to a degree. Tune into your target customer's expectations. Place the table with a direct view of the cooking areas and away from the dish room. An elevated booth can alter the perspective so diners are looking slightly down. Choose roomy seating for six to eight. Couples can be grouped together to create a social event.

- **Go totally upscale with a glass-enclosed air-conditioned balcony** with sound a system (to regulate kitchen noise).

- **Don't have room for a chef's table?** Perhaps you can incorporate a tour of the kitchen. Commander's Palace asks all diners if they'd like to leave through the kitchen to see the action. People relish the experience and even wait in line to go down a small back staircase.

First Impressions

An attractive "front door" is a powerful welcome and invitation to dine. A well-planned exterior invites passersby to stop, guides customers to well-lit entrances, and previews the good things to come. Here are some ideas for problem solving, mood setting and marketing:

Parking
- **Review the ease of access, traffic flow and available parking** when selecting a location. Don't forget to check local regulations and ADA requirements regarding accessibility for disabled customers.

- **Offer prominently located bike racks, convenient valet parking, free parking validation** or rickshaw/golf cart rides to and from distant lots during busy dinner hours.

- **Provide visible signage to "steer" customers to your front door.** Don't forget signs that announce and explain ways to make driving to, parking at and leaving your restaurant easier.

Waiting
- **Decide on whether you'll include exterior seating.** Know your target audience to determine whether long lines are a sign of a great hot spot or a signal that customers should go elsewhere for a quick meal.

- **Look for exterior seating materials that are easy to clean,** drain well, stay reasonably cool to the touch and won't snag or stain clothes or shed slivers.

- **Select chairs, benches or low "walls" that can be secured** for stability and reflect your interior style.

Mood Setting

- **Introduce diners to your theme in bold strokes** with playground equipment, oversized decorative sculptures, dramatic color schemes and fantasy environments.

- **Help differentiate your restaurant** from the monochromatic industrial looks of malls, strip centers and office buildings. Transform your entry with colorful awnings, fresh flower boxes, window displays, attractive murals and signs.

- **Add music,** piped through exterior speakers, to set the mood and stimulate appetites.

- **Post menus** and add "daily special" signage. These are great marketing tools to reinforce the decision to wait for a table or lure in potential customers passing by.

- **Greet customers with positive smells.** Fill your landscape with colorful and fragrant flowers, place freshly baked goods near exterior vents, and use pleasant-smelling cleaning products in entryways.

May I Take Your Coat?

An entryway can be as grand as a hotel lobby or merely a hallway. No matter how much open space you have available just inside the front door, use it wisely. Entry areas need functional and decorative features that make the waiting process less stressful and seem shorter. Your waiting area could include:

- **Comfortable seating with controlled temperatures.** Try not to freeze or bake customers every time the door opens.

- **Child activities.** Entertain the children with indoor play areas, arcade games and other activities. Offer small trinkets.

- **Signs which give seating and serving instructions.** For example: "Please Seat Yourself," "Our Hostess Will Seat You" and "Our Sumptuous Buffet Starts Here." Make sure that the host/hostess and cashier stations are clearly defined.

- **Traffic-control features.** Construct a well-placed wall, movable barriers, signs and railings. Also, pay phones, local publications and vending machines must be located in a convenient position.

- **Menus.** Introduce "daily special" bulletin boards and displays that sell what's to come. Have menus posted or hand them out. How about a decorative raw food display (e.g. whole salmons, fresh bread or imported cheeses). Display your desserts in the dining room. Offer a take-out service.

- **Retail items for sale.** For example, have a house specialty, stuffed animal mascot or after-dinner treat.

- **Décor as entertainment.** Introduce décor features that entertain, such as fish tanks, jukeboxes or local memorabilia.

- **Coatrooms.** Encourage your staff to assist customers with their coats. Whether your coatroom is a walk-in closet or a formal affair with an attendant, do your best to provide a sense of security and have an organized way to "file and retrieve" checked items. Restrict access whenever possible. Tag check-in items and hand out corresponding chips or receipts. Provide ample airflow to keep damp, cigarette/cigar and other smells from transferring. Use good-quality hangers to protect fragile sweaters, expensive furs and heavyweight coats.

Dining Alfresco

Outdoor dining can be a great way to expand seating areas, stimulate appetites, take advantage of natural views and entice others to join in for a good time. When considering an outdoor dining area, be certain to:

- **Review zoning regulations.** Check for possible restrictions, such as serving alcohol outdoors.

- **Look at the environment during morning, noon and evening hours.** Note whether ambient lighting from streetlights and nearby buildings is overly bright. Is the air quality good? Does the noise level make conversation difficult? Are there any other undesirable conditions that cannot be controlled, such as wind or unpleasant smells?

- **Watch the sun during daylight hours** to determine overly sunny and shadowy areas. Is the heat during lunchtime excessive? Are customers blinded by direct or reflective glare off tabletops, walk surfaces and nearby windows?

- **Consider whether food can be served quickly and easily** in an alfresco setting. Compute the distance from the kitchen. Create a flowchart to determine whether traffic patterns could create problems for servers carrying full trays.

Outwit environmental conditions and extend the outdoor dining season:
- **Strategically place plants, trees and decorative accents** to obscure unattractive views, shelter customers from the wind and soften noise levels.

- **Play soft music** to reduce traffic sounds and create a more intimate environment.

- **Provide ample and well-placed lighting** to read menus and ward off slip-and-fall injuries, without forsaking the desired atmosphere.

- **Warm chilly evenings** with portable gas heaters, fireplaces and fire pits.

- **Include a well-outfitted "wait station"** to help reduce trips to a distant kitchen, keep beverages hot and cold and shorten customer-request response times.

- **Tame Mother Nature and protect customers** from sunburns or sudden showers with well-secured umbrellas, patio covers, pergolas and awnings.

- **Control the environment.** Install trap fencing, low walls, shrubbery or other attractive barriers that direct people back through your main doorway. Physical barriers may also be a requirement when serving alcohol outdoors and can foil "dine and dash" events.

Colors That Compliment

When we say we had a great dining experience, we are referring to a combination of good food and an environment that put us in the right mood. Moods often dictate the type of food we seek out and where we eat it. Creating the right mood means using proper design elements and more subtle factors that affect humans psychologically.

Colors and moods
- **Scientists have proven** that people are affected by the colors surrounding them. Why not incorporate one or two to create the right mood for your restaurant?

- **Yellow.** Sunlight, cheerful, vitality. Many designers believe every room should have a dash of yellow. Stay away from greenish yellows.

- **Red.** Intensity, passion, stimulates appetites. Use boldly or as an accent.

- **Blue.** Cool, clean and refreshing. Blue should be used away from food, as it isn't complementary.

- **Green.** Well-being, nature, fresh and light. Beware - can also make people and food look off-color.

- **Gold.** Wealth and power. Warms up other colors and brightens dark wood.

- **Neutrals.** Masculine - darker browns. Feminine - lighter terra cotta shades. Rosy hues make food and people more attractive, rarely go out of style and provide a background for bold color accents.

- **White.** Clean, fresh and new. Can be a good foundation color, but beware - it can also signal institutional, bland, ordinary. Can create glare and eyestrain and be hard to maintain.

- **Black.** Death and mourning. However, used properly, black can add elegance and style. Black and white is a classic look. Avoid as a background color unless you are creating a nightclub or are using unique colored lighting. Don't forget that black can show finger and foot prints and can be difficult to keep looking clean.

The Ancient Art of Feng Shui

Feng Shui (say fung shway) is the Chinese art form dealing with the proper placement of buildings (homes or businesses) and the elements within and how they can positively and negatively affect human behavior and fortunes. Whether you are an ardent believer or merely curious, Feng Shui offers some sound design principles. Here are a few areas that Feng Shui addresses:

- **Seating.** It is considered bad Feng Shui to have your back to an entryway because enemies could surprise you. The design translation: sitting with your back to the door makes you feel uncomfortable.

- **Mirrors.** Should reflect beautiful views (not glimpses of hallways and storage areas).

- **Colors.** Colors should be used in specific areas of the building to create specific positive influences, actions and fortunes.

- **Activities.** All buildings are divided into areas where specific activities should take place. For example, your office should be placed in the building's money area.

- **Organization.** Clutter causes distress and chaos. Busy restaurants can benefit from the organizational aspects of Feng Shui.

- **Hire a Feng Shui advisor** to bring customers (and good luck and money) into your restaurant. Try the Western School of Feng Shui directory at www.wsfs.com/statesdirectory.htm or a national directory site such as www.fengshuidirectory.com to find a local consultant.

- **Pick up a couple of books.** Review the principles, which work for home or business. Popular author Lillian Too has written over 50 Feng Shui books and Amazon.com lists over 400 books on the subject.

- **Visit the *World of Feng Shui* online magazine** at www.wofs.com or *Feng Shui Times* at www.feng-shuitimes.com.

- **Ask your architect and design consultants about this "hot" design topic.** Many tradition-based creative professionals are adding Feng Shui to their skills.

Add a Touch of Green

Greenery and flowering plants, inside and outside your restaurant, are great decorative touches that add life and vitality to an environment. Interior plants can even help filter the air and provide additional oxygen. Attractive landscaping can brighten a dull environment, hide unattractive exterior elements (such as garbage areas, adjacent buildings or freeways), create an entryway focal point or provide a cool area to wait. When incorporating plants into your restaurant design and décor, remember that they require adequate light, moisture and accessibility. The following are some plant décor and landscaping hints for those without a green thumb:

- **Hire a plant maintenance or landscape firm** to keep everything trimmed, fed and looking fresh. Dead or spindly plants and yellowed leaves lying about are unappetizing signals to guests. Rotate interior plants regularly. Make certain the plants look good year-round or can be inexpensively removed and replaced with more seasonally suitable choices.

- **Add non-plant elements.** Attractive tiles, fishponds, flags, sculpture, fountains, dry creek beds, ambient lighting and birdbaths can decorate parking lots, entries and waiting areas.

- **Go faux!** Silk plants may be a better choice under some conditions. Select top-quality artificial plants with flowers and leaves in natural colors. Bright blue blossoms may coordinate with your décor but they aren't frequently found in nature.

- **Create portable flower gardens.** Use colorful pots, planters, hanging baskets, barrels or even old kitchen items. These can be great ways to soften hardscapes.

- **Unattractive plants.** Avoid plants that are unpleasant smelling, have prickly needles, leaves or thorns or have toxic leaves, flowers or berries.

- **Select the right plant for the space.** Consider light and watering requirements and full-growth size. Don't let vines dangle in someone's face or let upright plants interrupt an attractive dining room view. Use full-spectrum lights for healthier indoor plants. Have plant shelves installed with drains and incorporate hanging plants using a retracting or track system.

- **Place water faucets (interior and exterior) near areas that will have trees and large plants** that require lots of water. Include plants that create "fresh air" to purify indoor air. To learn more about healthy air plants, read the section on indoor air quality, "The Air We Breathe."

Commissioning Artists

Finding the right artwork for your restaurant may mean that you have to commission an artist to create the perfect piece. Hiring an artist isn't like hiring any other professional. What constitutes "art" is in the eye of the beholder and can frequently be difficult to define. Working closely with an artist during the conceptualization stage is critical. You or your interior decorator may choose to commission visual art such as a mural, an oil painting, a kinetic sculpture, a fountain, a stained glass window, photographs, metalwork, woodcarvings, ceramics or glassware. Musical artists can also be commissioned to create customized background music or create original compositions. Bear in mind the following:

- **Discussion.** Discuss your concept in detail, including size, installation requirements, budget and production timetable. Allow the artist to maintain the creative spirit. When commissioning a project, remember, overly coordinated mass-produced art isn't your goal.

- **Review the artist's portfolio.** Examples of the artist's work can stimulate ideas and eliminate things that you don't like. Choose the right artist for the project. Artistic style and experience, along with your personal chemistry, are important.

- **Preview.** Ask whether initial sketches, models or other preliminary design work can be previewed before expensive materials are purchased or too much time passes.

- **Your target audience.** Communicate your restaurant's theme, design notes, ideal customer profile and other information that can give the artist more background and stimuli from which to draw.

- **Invest in good frames, target lighting and proper display areas.** Showcase the artist's efforts for maximum effect.

- **Develop relationships with local artists** where featured artwork is rotated regularly to give your public areas fresh new looks. This can be a great cost-effective way to help the artist and your business. Tasteful signage should be provided with details about the artist and subject matter.

Music to Stimulate, Soothe and Woo

Whether you want to mask kitchen noises, create a romantic environment or stimulate appetites, music can enhance your restaurant's bottom line. Properly selected background music builds upon your restaurant theme and brand and helps draw in specific customers. Like many restaurant features, it's best to incorporate music system needs in the early budgeting and design stages. The following offer some useful ideas for adding musical enhancements to your restaurant:

- **Hire a commercial music system specialist.** Ask him or her to assess your building's acoustics, develop a properly balanced system and block irritating noises.

- **Select a system that meets your budget** and customer quality expectations. Installed commercial music systems range from $0.75 to $10 per square foot (pricing information from JBL Pro at www.jblpro.com). Discriminating adults will have higher standards than preteens.

- **Ask about upgradability and volume capabilities** (loud = distortion free; soft = full tones). Explore options; e.g., would an "off-the-shelf" or custom system would be more appropriate?

- **Paging.** Incorporate your paging needs to ensure staff and patrons can clearly hear pages and announcements without sacrificing music quality.

- **Check out your cable or satellite TV provider for commercial music options.** You may not need to set up a separate system. Digital Music Express, DMX at www.dmxmusic.com, offers over 100 CD-quality music channels through 800+ cable TV providers and direct satellite systems.

- **Remember the fees.** Businesses are legally required to pay music-licensing fees (even if your only music is a radio). Companies like Award-Winning Music at www.royaltyfreemusic.com can supply royalty-free music and eliminate this fee.

- **Create a sound-positive music niche away from dining room traffic lanes for piano or harp soloists.** Provide adjustable mood and spotlights and build in conveniently located electrical outlets and music system plug-ins. The flooring and substructure should be able to handle heavy instruments (up to 1,000 pounds for a grand piano). Have your designer incorporate background speakers to avoid the ugly "black box" look.

- **Don't overlook music in the kitchen and staff areas.** Music is proven to enhance productivity and reduce stress. Just make certain that it doesn't overwhelm normal voice-level conversation or conflict with your dining room ambiance.

Let There Be Light

Lighting is more than a chandelier here and a lamp there. Well-designed lighting creates a mood, enhances décor, makes it easier and safer to work and makes diners and their food look better. When considering how to light your dining area, here are some things you will have to bear in mind:

Take a long, hard look at your establishment. Consider these factors:
- **Level of natural light** and seasonal changes that affect it.

- **Activities within the room** - work areas, walkways, tables, waiting areas.

- **Ambiance you wish to create** - bright and stimulating or soft and romantic.

- **Artistic and creative uses** - the use of light and shadows to accent attractive features or mask "ugly" areas.

- **Lighting effects.** These can be obtained through wall sconces, fiber optics, chandeliers, track lighting, table lamps, directional spotlights and even candles. Incorporate indirect lighting. Well-placed wall sconces add light without the glare.

- **Install dimmers** to adjust your lighting levels by the time of day. Lunchtime lighting should be brighter than evening lighting. Don't mistake a dim room for an elegant or romantic room. Dining is a social experience and good lighting should enhance that.

- **Use color-accurate table lighting** to enhance the taste of food. Our sense of taste is affected by what our eyes see. Table lighting should softly accent the food, the china and the diners.

- **Choose lighting that enhances a color scheme.** Incandescent lighting has a warmer, yellow-orange cast; fluorescent lighting produces a blue-green cast, which is a real appetite deadener! Halogen lights are closest to true white light.

- **Explore full-spectrum lighting** (which reportedly makes people feel healthier) for work areas and plant displays.

- **Create a balance within the room.** Overly bright areas next to dim rooms are a distraction and create eye-adjustment problems.

- **Invest in automation for complex lighting systems.** Companies like Lutron Electronics, 800-523-9466, www.lutron.com, offer a variety of preset lighting control systems.

- **Hire a lighting designer.** This lighting expert can help you upgrade existing lighting for appearance and energy savings or design a complete new look. Alternatively, visit GE Lighting online at www.gelighting.com/na/business/restaurant_solutions . html for design, product selection and energy audits.

Ceilings

Ceilings are often overlooked when designing and decorating a restaurant. Diners actually do notice attractive colors, artistic displays and great lighting along with all the dust, cobwebs, stains and ugly ceiling materials. Attractive and clean ceilings tell customers that you value cleanliness throughout your restaurant. Here are some things you should know about choosing ceiling materials, designing unique ceilings and maintaining ceilings:

- **Look for sound-deadening materials.** Your choice must be easy to clean and easy to secure tightly to beams, sheetrock or suspension hardware.

- **Use moistureproof, mildew-resistant materials.** Materials on ceilings in high-moisture areas (food prep, dishwashing and restroom areas) must meet your local sanitary standards.

- **Transform ceilings with wallpaper, wood paneling, fabric** or other suspended treatments. Just be certain that all materials are flame-resistant and meet code.

- **Use exposed beams, pipes and vents as great color accents** and high-tech art pieces. Make certain paint and other treatments are fireproof and heat-resistant for heating and steam pipes, and waterproof for water pipes.

- **Reflect more light and make the room feel larger with lighter-colored ceilings.** Remember, lighter-colored ceilings will also show venting-related dirt stains. Your local Health Department may require light ceilings in work areas to aid inspectors.

- **Make certain your HVAC is properly vented and well maintained** to eliminate ceiling stains. Lack of maintenance isn't just unsightly; it also wastes electricity.

- **Natural light.** Incorporate skylights, light tubes and windows to bring in more natural light. Make certain these can be easily cleaned at least once a quarter.

- **Think of your ceiling as another wall to be decorated.** Tin ceilings, "faux" painting techniques, mirrors, posters, faux beams, decorative molding and fabric are all potential ways to add drama, carry out a theme or enhance a peaceful environment. Search for unique ceiling materials from architectural salvage yards.

Covering Your Floors

Although people might not gush about your flooring, it certainly influences their overall impressions of your restaurant and your restaurant's atmosphere. In a busy environment with heavy foot traffic, flooring choices have lasting consequences and can overwhelm your construction or renovation budget. Here are a few facts you should consider when selecting flooring materials:

- **Hard-wearing.** Choose commercial grade whenever possible as anticipated usage and lifespan are typically much greater. Research commercial flooring, including hardwood flooring at Floor You at www.flooryou.com.

Select materials for public areas that:
- Won't show scuff marks easily.
- Can handle chairs or equipment being dragged or wheeled over them.
- Won't be dented by high heels.
- Have a medium-colored pattern to hide spots, crumbs and dirt between cleanings.

- **Warranties.** Check all manufacturers' warranties for coverage in commercial environments.

- **Compare hardwood flooring with modern vinyl or acrylic-infused look-alikes.** Remember, wood can be sanded and refinished easily, while the look-alike would need to be replaced. Select the more expensive strip vinyl flooring for a longer life expectancy than other vinyl products. The ability to replace small damaged areas is an added benefit.

- **Ask your architect about the great ways that concrete can be used** in commercial buildings. New processes and color techniques make this an attractive and durable choice.

- **Explore more unusual flooring such as cork and bamboo.** These green products have unique looks and are great high-traffic choices.

- **Avoid dark, high-gloss flooring**, which can appear wavy and magnify any substructure imperfections.

Make certain all flooring is:
- Easy to maintain.
- Durable and stain-resistant.
- Slip-resistant in wet and dry conditions.
- Code approved for food prep areas.

The following charts contain some of the various flooring materials you might consider and their positive and negative features. The cost factors are broad ranges based on average retail price points. Please remember, quality levels vary greatly within each category and availability of commercial grades may be a factor. Installation costs are not included in these broad estimates.

Material	Cost Per Sq. Ft.	Life (Years)
Concrete	$1.00 to $5.50	10+

Positives/Negatives: Paint & seal to simulate more expensive materials. Loud & hard walk surface. Too stark or high-tech for some. May crack.

Vinyl, tile squares	$1.25 to $6.00	8 – 10

Positives/Negatives: Comfortable walk surface. Various colors & designs. Can create patterns. Grime where tiles meet. Can show wear. Not grease resistant. Limited commercial choices. Frequent maintenance.

Vinyl, sheet	$2.00 to $6.00	10 – 15

Positives/Negatives: Various colors & designs. Wide widths. Ordinary looking. Not grease resistant. Shows traffic wear. Hard to clean seams.

Cork	$3.25 to $10.00	15+

Positives/Negatives: Great for high-moisture areas. Sound deadening & resilient. Available in tiles, sheets & planks. Up to 10-year warranty. Limited U.S. commercial history.

Bamboo	$4.00 to $8.00	5 – 15

Positives/Negatives: Can be finished in a variety of stains & sealers. Durable (harder than red maple) & resilient. Some manufacturers offer lifetime structural warranties. Can be refinished like wood. Refer to manufacturer's warranty. Wear warranty typically 5 years. Limited U.S. commercial history.

Ceramic Tile	$4.00 to $15.00	20+

Positives/Negatives: Can add color or elegance depending upon tile size, layout & design. Mosaic designs are very hot now. Doesn't easily "wear out." Slippery. Loud & hard walk surface. Can be chipped, broken easily. Grout may discolor.

Slate	$5.00 to $12.00	10+

Positives/Negatives: Natural, elegant look. Never "wears out." Very porous. Limited colors. Loud & hard walk surface.

Material	Cost Per Sq. Ft.	Life (Years)
Carpet, olefin	$.95 to $2.00	2

Positives/Negatives: Least-expensive carpet choice. Softer walk surface. Turns ugly quickly. Absorbs grease.

Carpet, nylon	$1.60 to $4.59	3 – 7

Positives/Negatives: Variety of colors, textures & thicknesses. Durable, easy to clean. Good sound deadening. Quality levels vary significantly.

Carpet, wool	$3.80 to $12.00	7 – 10

Positives/Negatives: Longest-lasting carpet. Intricate designs & rich colors say "elegant." Harder to maintain. May shrink when wet.

Marble	$8.00 to $25.00	20+

Positives/Negatives: Elegant looks. Very slippery, porous, stains easily. Hard & loud walk surface. Requires polishing & refinishing.

Granite	$12.00 to $30.00	20+

Positives/Negatives: Elegant looks. Less porous than marble. Limited colors.

Wood	$5.00 to $30.00	varies

Positives/Negatives: Life varies by species (select the hardest wood you can afford). Warm, upscale look. Hides soil. Good walk surface. Less noisy. Needs periodic refinishing. Finish may peel or wear poorly. Heels & table legs can dent wood.

Wood, simulate (vinyl laminates)	$3.75 to $40.00	5-to-25 year warranty

Positives/Negatives: High-end appearance with low maintenance. Variety of wood looks. Requires level subsurface. Quality varies by manufacturer.

Seating

You won't be profitable if you don't have enough seats or cannot turn them quickly enough. This means creating an environment where people can find a seat when they want it, rest comfortably and have ample elbowroom - and will leave when you want them to. Your goal in choosing your dining room seating is to balance beauty, functionality and psychological factors. Your seating choices add decorative elements to the room, dictate the traffic/work flow and signal diners to the upcoming experience. Proper seating can help your waitstaff to serve patrons more quickly and efficiently.

When choosing seating, remember to choose chairs that:

- Are easy to move, stack and store.
- Provide plenty of elbowroom and don't forget left-handed customers.
- Don't overlook solo diners. Have plenty of suitable deuces (tables for two) in good locations and have a communal table for those craving some company.
- Select chairs that are of appropriate height in relationship to the table. Is the legroom sufficient without making shorter adult diners feel like children? Supply sturdy chairs for larger folks and booths, where shorter customers can easily reach their plates.

- **Durability.** Purchase sturdy, stable seating that can handle the wear-and-tear of a busy restaurant.

- **Consider your customers.** Opt for swivels, wheels, glider pads and other enhancements to make sitting down easier. Or, customize wooden chairs with chair pads. Remember, elderly and handicapped patrons may need roomier access.

- **Supply high chairs** that can slide close to tables and booster seats that fit your chairs and/or benches.

- **Don't forget that you may want to use your chairs for alfresco dining options.** Choose materials that don't tarnish when exposed to the sun.

- **Hire a restaurant consultant with experience in seating design and layout.** They can help you calculate the profit potential of your seating. This is critical when expanding your seating to ensure that the ROI is significant enough to offset your costs.

Selecting Tables

Unless you are a drive-up-only establishment, your guests will need a table to gather around. The following offer some practical tips on table selection:

- **Determine whether your tables will be visible or covered.** You'll save plenty on less attractive, yet practical, surfaces if tablecloths hide them.

- **Choose light-colored tabletops** if you are using white or pale tablecloths.

- **Confirm that tabletop surfaces are waterproof.** Sealants or a glass top can be added to less durable surfaces.

- **Look for self-leveling legs/bases** to compensate for uneven flooring.

- **Think of your tables as decorative opportunities.** Unusual legs, eye-popping colors and creative mosaics can be incorporated. Paper items (old calendars, cocktail napkins) can be displayed under urethane sealer or a glass top.

- **Review your customer makeup and mix and match tables.** Factor in guests with books, newspapers and briefcases and solo diners preferring larger tables.

1 – 2 guests (2-top) ....24-in. by 30-in. square.
3 – 4 guests (4-top) ....36-in. by 36-in. square
                                   30-in. by 48-in. rectangle
                                   42-in. round.
5 – 6 guests ....2-top and 4-top joined
                                   48-in. or 54-in. round
7 – 8 guests...................................Joined two 4-tops
                                   72-in. round

- **Purchase tables with uniform heights and widths** for easier grouping and chair compatibility. Purchase tops and bases separately for additional flexibility and easier storage.

- **Consider your customers' size.** Larger customers may feel cramped at smaller tables. Likewise, oversized booths can make it hard for shorter customers to sit within reach of drinks, condiments, etc.

For disabled customers:
- **Purchase tables with a height of 27-inches high by 30-inches wide by 19-inches deep.**

- **Examine booth** ends for support legs that won't interfere with wheelchairs.

- **Set up a typical table setting for your restaurant** to compute accurate table size. An average place setting is 24-inches wide. Don't forget to allow for trays in self-service situations.

- **Select booths with freestanding tables.** You'll be able to shift these to accommodate smaller or larger guests.

- **Add a lazy Susan to large round tables** for condiments and family-style dining.

Seating as Décor

From '50s retro vinyl to high-tech banquettes to wingback chairs, the seats you offer your customers should reflect your dining room design or theme. Your food service style has a direct impact on the type of eating and sitting surfaces that you provide. Here are some popular choices for seating, based on your service style: Choose the type of seating that will compliment your décor. Consider which category is most appropriate for your establishment:

- **Fast-food.** For outdoors, choose picnic-table-style seating with benches and cover umbrellas. For indoors, choose counters with stools for diners, bench-table combination, booths and banquettes. Take-out? Choose chairs for waiting only. Focus on hard-surface seating (concrete, molded plastic, vinyl) that can handle heavy traffic, cleans easily and encourages quick turns.

- **Cafeteria/buffet.** Seating geared at easy access. Freestanding tables and chairs with ample walk space. Tables and carpets designed for heavy traffic and easy cleaning.

- **Sit-down.** A combination of seating could be provided to accommodate diners who prefer the privacy of a booth or the visibility of a centrally located table. Understanding your ideal customer will help you choose which such a customer would most typically prefer.

- **Family restaurants.** There's plenty to choose from, when it comes to family-style restaurants. Just be certain to select sizes and materials suitable for busy kids.

- **Formal dining.** Formal restaurants will typically include more soft surfaces, which are considered more luxurious. Colors would be more muted and elegant.

Your Profit Center

Filling and turning seats is your primary profit center. Ample capacity means greater profit potential. Your seating (table and chair choices) also can directly affect your pocketbook, from the initial purchase to the room layout to upkeep. You need to be able to accommodate sufficient customers on an hourly, weekly and monthly basis to pay for overhead and food and post a profit. Turning tables quickly is especially critical in high-volume, low-margin operations. Here are some profit-motive suggestions you should consider:

- **Compute your average check size.** Figure out how extra seats might mean great profits. For example, bulky barrel-shaped chairs fit your décor but require more space. Smaller seating allows you to serve ten more people for lunch. If your average ticket is $12, you take in an extra $120 per lunch shift and over $2,500 extra per month.

- **Figure out how many customers you'll need to seat during peak times.** Work at minimizing wait times and increasing your potential to serve more people per hour with ample seating.

- **Don't make it too comfortable.** If your goal is a quick turnover, use more rigid seating to subtly discourage lingering.

- **Help your servers.** Table layout can affect the speed in which diners are served. If faster service is your goal, make certain servers aren't battling your table placement.

- **Help your bus person.** Again, if speed is of the essence, don't use fussy tablecloths and napkins, and make certain surfaces can be cleaned quickly and efficiently.

Seating as Work (and Play) Areas

You should also consider the ergonomics of your chosen seating and dining area layout. For more information on how customers and staff interact with physical objects, read the section on ergonomics. Here are some practical ideas you should consider that will enhance the dining experience and improve server performance.

Determine the activities your customers and staff will be doing at the table.

- Will salads or desserts be prepared and served tableside?

- Will diners wish to use their laptops for business, read the morning paper or feed small children?

- Will diners be cooking or preparing their own food? Dipping bread into a fondue pot or assembling a taco?

- Will people want a view of your stage or other focal point?

- **Review how well servers can quickly and easily reach each diner**. Will they be forced to hoist heavy bowls or drink trays over a patron's head? Does a maze exist, or will food come directly from the kitchen?

- **Make certain staff can rearrange tables quickly and easily** to accommodate the party's size. Can you quickly create a cozy table for 2 or seating for 15?

- **Don't forget to allow for tabletop accessories** (napkins, salt and pepper) and marketing items (dessert or drink specials). Can the table accommodate oversized place mats, plates or glassware? Will silverware for multi-course presentations be well displayed? Will diners need room for fondue pots, fajita platters or food warmers?

Acting as Your Own Decorator

Many entrepreneurs enjoy the creative process of decorating with or without professional help. Some projects aren't large enough to warrant the services of an interior design consultant. Perhaps you are simply seeking concept ideas. The following are some valuable national resources for restaurant décor:

Company Name	Web/Phone
Décor Item: Limited to your imagination	
eBay (auction site)	www.ebay.com
Décor Item: Antique architectural elements	
Architectural Antiques (Denver & Minneapolis)	www.archantiques.com
Décor Item: Antique lighting	
Antique Lighting	www.antique-lighting.com
Décor Item: Everything from rugs to columns	
Interior Mall	www.interiormall.com 800-590-5844
Décor Item: Giclee canvas, framed art	
Ariel of France	www.arieloffrance.com 713-460-4100
Décor Item: Robots	
Robot Factory	www.robotfactory.com
Décor Item: Nautical décor	
ARE Restaurant Equipment	www.amer-rest-equip.com /deco/are_decoindex.html
Décor Item: Fiberglass mounted fish	
King Sailfish Mounts	www.kingsailfish.com

Company Name	Web/Phone

Décor Item: Restoration/decorative hardware

Crown City Hardware
www.crowncityhardware.com
800-950-1047

Décor Item: Plastic food replicas & menu-oriented displays

Fax Food
www.faxfoods.com
800-929-1189

Décor Item: Antique hardware

Liz's Antique Hardware
www.lahardware.com

Décor Item: Sports décor

Sports Expressions
www.sportsexpressions.com
480-596-1913

Décor Item: Posters, vintage food ads

Bare Walls
www.barewalls.com/indexes/b2brest.html
800-455-3955

Décor Item: Vintage neon & signs

Roadhouse Relics
www.roadhouserelics.com
512-442-NEON

Décor Item: Reclaimed lumber

Historic Lumber
www.historiclumber.ca/restaurant.htm
519-853-0008

Décor Item: Southern décor, antiques

Anything Southern
www.anythingsourthern.com

Décor Item: Celtic pub items

Celtic Dragon Pub Co.
www.celticdragonpubco.com
321-459-2775

Décor Item: Hawaiian & tiki

Tiki Traders
www.tikitrader.com

Company Name	Web/Phone
Décor Item: Antique cash registers & drug store memorabilia	
National Brass	www.nationalbrass.com
Décor Item: Colorful custom tabletops	
The Furniture Lab	www.homeontherange.com/ restaurants/restaurants_index.html
Décor Item: Celebrity memorabilia	
Startifacts	www.startifacts.com
Décor Item: Neon	
Neonetics	www.neonetics.com
Décor Item: Cowboy & Mexican	
El Paso Saddle Blanket	www.elpasosaddleblanket.com
Décor Item: "Tiffany" lamps	
Meyda	www.meyda.com
Décor Item: Animated displays	
Characters Unlimited	www.charactersunlimitedinc.com 702-294-0563

A few suggestions for sourcing innovative decorative items:

- **Architectural salvage yards** – old gates, wrought iron fencing, arches, pillars, signs, windows.

- **Flea markets and antique stores.** Find lots of ideas for trash-to-treasure, such as collectable glassware to integrate with your fine china, old food advertising and old kitchen items.

- **Aquarium stores.** Integrating fresh- or salt-water fish can make a colorful addition.

- **Garden shops -** fountains, live plants. Bring outdoor garden items like arbors, lattices and seed packages inside.

- **Craft stores -** artificial plants, decoupage, glass etchings.

- **Paint supply** - faux painting supplies and techniques. Paint is a versatile and inexpensive decorative tool.

- **Kitchen shops, home décor stores.** Walk up and down the aisles looking for new and creative ways to incorporate ordinary items into your décor.

The Smallest Room in the House

Restrooms may be the smallest rooms in the house but they are important ones for guests. An ample, clean restroom speaks loudly about how you value cleanliness and are considerate of guests' needs. Plumbing and Health Department standards vary widely across the U.S. Also, the Americans with Disabilities Act (ADA) governs accessibility issues for all public places. Be certain that you comply, as inadequate restrooms can keep you from opening for business. Here are some practical and creative ideas on designing and decorating restrooms:

- **Locate them with easy access.** Depending upon your plumbing layout, restrooms can be up front, so guests can enter before moving into the dining room, or tucked back out of view. For their children's safety, many parents would prefer restroom entrances that are visible from the dining area.

- **Remember your customers' physical needs.** Provide sinks, dryers and dispensers at levels appropriate for children and wheelchair-bound patrons. For ADA advice, call the U.S. Department of Justice at 800-514-0301.

- **Plan on ample restroom capacity.**

- **Small restaurants (up to 50 seats) should allot at least a 35- to 40-square-foot area for one toilet** and a washbasin.

- **Create a room that reflects the front-of-the-house.** The more elegant the restaurant, the more spacious and elegant the restroom.

- **Select materials that wear well,** won't show dirt and can handle strong cleaners. Ceramic tile is great but be aware of grout discoloration.

- **Remember that more automated is better.** People dislike touching bathroom surfaces, and automation conserves water and electricity.

Make your female customers happy with:
- **Extra square footage and more stalls.** Women expect more privacy and have to deal with more carry-in items (purses, strollers) and small children.

- **Adequate and flattering lighting and mirrors by which** to touch up makeup and hair.

- **A separate, clean nursing area** with comfortable seating. Would you like to eat in a typical washroom?

- **Avoid public unisex rooms whenever possible.** This may be a practical solution and "politically correct," but most people still feel uncomfortable. Also, some jurisdictions require separate facilities for men and women. The exception to this is the thoughtful addition of an oversized "parent and child" restroom.

- **Staff facilities**. Provide separate facilities for staff if possible.

Front-of-the-House Support Stations

Realistically, not all food prep and service work can be accomplished behind closed doors. To do so would exhaust your waitstaff unnecessarily, slow down your service and create a workflow nightmare in the back-of-the house. Consider the following options:

- **Work stations.** Depending upon your restaurant layout, service methods, etc., some workstations could have multiple functions. Here are some different types of workstations you might need in the front-of-the-house:

  - **Reception.** Meet and greet, take reservations, assign customers to servers.

  - **Computerization** - point-of-sale ordering centers, item availability and inventory control.

  - **Cashiering.** Ring up and accept payments, process credit card charges, sell retail items.

  - **Food service** - beverage centers, salad prep area, dessert service.

  - **Dinnerware and utensil storage** - storage for place settings, additional napkins, specialty utensils.

  - **Support stations.** Here are some helpful suggestions on designing and implementing front-of-the-house support stations:

  - **Make them attractive.** Support stations can be camouflaged with decorative panels and plants or designed to be a part of the "show."

  - **Remember, cleanliness and orderliness are required** when service personnel prepare food in full view of guests. Hide all the extra equipment and supplies behind doors.

- **Don't forget to build in floor drains,** use scuff-resistant baseboards and add casters to equipment that must be moved for cleaning.

- **Reduce lifting and carrying** with mobile carts and rolling waste receptacles.

- **Use properly aimed task lighting** to avoid glare while allowing staff full visibility of the work surface.

- **Use antifatigue mats and nonslip flooring.**

- **Design work areas to minimize stooping, reaching and lifting.**

- **Run computer network, phone and electrical wiring to each workstation.**

- **Separate "wet" and "dry" tasks** to avoid damage, food contamination and electrical accidents.

- **Incorporate hand and/or utility sinks** wherever possible to save steps and promote cleanliness.

- **Provide ample counter space** below pass-throughs to add garnishes, verify orders and fill trays.

- **Consider including a small (and quiet) under-counter glass washer** for thorough cleanup of critical tools and utensils.

CHAPTER SEVEN

BACK-OF-THE-HOUSE

Streamline Your Activities Back-of-the-House

The "show" may be up front – but its driving force is behind the swinging doors. A well-designed and properly outfitted back-of-the-house combines three elements: ergonomics, efficiency and economy:

Ergonomics

Create a worker-friendly environment that protects your employees and improves attitudes. For more information on ergonomics, see chapter 4, "Environmental and Safety Issues." Also, ask yourself the following questions about each piece of equipment:

- Are the control knobs, levels, on/off switches or other critical components placed within easy reach?

- Can shorter or left-handed employees safely use it?

- Are people walking through a maze of equipment and worktables?

- Is the height accurate for sitting, standing or reaching?

- Can people easily move the object to use or clean it?

- Can a different layout, material or design make it easier on the operator's body?

- Can a piece of equipment or better tool reduce repetitive stress injuries?

Efficiency

Remember, efficiency translates directly into time, and time is money. When selecting tools, fixtures and equipment and establishing layouts, you should always weigh the ability to produce more or save more against the initial cost. For example, a more efficient dishwasher might cost more initially; however, the ROI translates into reduced waits for clean dishes, lower dependence on employees and fewer plates to purchase. Ask yourself the following questions before making any kitchen design or purchasing decisions:

- Does the item make a task easier or reduce labor costs? An electric slicer, for example, versus hand-slicing.

- Can one piece of equipment be used for multiple types of tasks? How about a mixer with grinder or slicer attachments?

- Are the features easy to use? Will people abandon the "time-saving" features because they don't understand them or get frustrated when operating them?

- Does it improve serving times or the quality of your service? This could be a computerized ordering system or direct access to finishing and holding areas.

Economy

Whether upgrading or outfitting a new back-of-the-house, it's rare that you'll have an unlimited budget. Besides, why overspend unnecessarily? Economically sound decisions can improve your profit potential and save you thousands over the life of your business. Overspending takes money out of your pocket that you never recover. When considering the financial impact of designs, tools, fixtures and equipment, don't forget to:

- **Compare lifetime costs.** Factor in costs for energy, maintenance, cleaning and consumables (filters, ink cartridges, specialty paper). Factor in labor savings through reduced overtime or fewer employees.

• **Consider upgrade capabilities and costs** should you need something bigger, better, faster, harder.

• **Review trade-in allowances, potential rebates, low-interest loans and special offerings** by utility companies, manufacturers and distributors.

• **Save steps whenever possible.** There is a direct correlation between the economy of movement and productivity. Shaving even a few seconds off service times can increase your profit margin and make customers happier.

Fixtures and Equipment

Outfitting your kitchen and public areas requires purchasing a variety of fixtures and equipment used to prepare, store and display raw and finished products. Fixtures such as glass display cases and miscellaneous "non-cooking" equipment, such as carts and racks, can quickly eat up your budget. Unless the fixture is a moneymaker (such as a retail display case), don't go overboard on these. Here are some resources and practical tips on purchasing fixtures and equipment for your restaurant:

Shop online directories for local and regional suppliers:
• **Power Sourcing**: www.powersourcing.com/se/restaurantfixturesequipment.htm
• **Foodservice Central**: www.foodservicecentral.com
• **Foodservice.com**: www.foodservice.com
• **Restaurant Operator**: www.restaurantoperator.com
• **FoodServiceSearch.com**: www.foodservicesearch.com
• **SEFA (Supply and Equipment Foodservice Alliance)**: www.sefa.com
• **Food Service Equipment Reports Magazine:** www.fermag.com

- **Business.com** (search engine): www.business.com/directory/food_and_beverage/restaurants_and_foodservice/equipment_and_supplies.

Kitchen Design

Poorly designed kitchens and equipment are a major complaint of busy chefs and assistants. Poor planning decreases productivity, increases wait times, contributes to employee turnover and distracts busy workers. Whether you are a chef-owner or just share the vision of a talented chef, your attention to food quality and prompt service relies on the efficiency of a properly outfitted kitchen. Good kitchen design is an art and a science. Here's where an experienced consultant comes in handy – to balance space limitations, safety issues, food prep needs and budgets without sacrificing food quality, productivity and your staff's sanity!

- **Your menu directly affects your kitchen design.** Take a look at the suggestions outlined in the section "What's on the Menu?" before you make any design decisions. What you'll serve (raw ingredients and prepared foods) and how you'll serve it determine your needs for prep, assembly, storage and serving.

- **Workflow.** There are several different workflow patterns that can be used to create a balance between passive storage and active work areas. You'll need areas to accommodate for:
  - **Hot and cold foods** - prep and assembly
  - **Beverage** - dispensing and storage
  - **Storage** - food and non-food items
  - **Sanitation** - ware washing and front-of-the-house cleaning equipment and supplies
  - **Receiving** - off-loading space and inventory systems

Your Chef's Office

Here are some suggestions on how you might make your kitchen layout work for your chef and support staff:

- **Break your kitchen activities into self-contained workstations.** Make sure that ingredients, tools, equipment, supplies and preserving storage are within easy reach.

- **Create work triangles.** Triangle or diamond layouts give quick access to prep tables, sinks and cooking equipment. Straight-line layouts work best for assembly line-style prep and cooking where more than one person participates.

- **Draw out traffic maps.** Minimize unnecessary steps and crisscrossing paths.

- **Locate your cooking and final prep areas closest to the dining room.** Keep food temperatures accurate.

- **Consider placing your volume or batch cooking areas towards the back of the kitchen** and your to-order needs nearest the dining room. Production that requires little tending shouldn't take up precious high-activity space.

- **Isolate dishwashing tasks.** The noises and chemical smell shouldn't mingle with your dining room ambiance.

- **Allow for ample open space.** People need to pass, carts need to be rolled, shelving moved, large buckets wheeled and trays lifted.

- **Coordinate placement of all equipment that requires venting** to share a single ventilation system and reduce costs. Check your local code requirements on ventilation of heat- and moisture-producing equipment.

- **Include plenty of waste receptacles.** Divide by type of waste if you will be implementing recycling programs. Check with your waste management company on local requirements for segregating glass, metal, paper, etc.

- **Design kitchens with multiple sets of "in" and "out" doors.** Examples: doors that go directly from the dining area to the dish room (bypassing food prep); doors from the bar to the dish room, ice machine and/or barware and liquor storage.

- **Ask your staff.** Take advantage of their daily experiences and enhance their work areas during a kitchen renovation.

- **Take a look at the workflow advice** in chapter 3, "Construction and Renovation."

Plenty of Storage

You'll never hear anyone complain about too much storage. This is especially true about storing costly perishables, organizing unwieldy linens and fragile dishes, buying in quantity and warehousing seasonal décor. Well-designed storage creates a safer work environment, encourages productivity, decreases clutter and saves you money. Here are some practical ideas on creating useful storage areas.

Increase productivity by creating three types of storage:

- **Active** - accessed repeatedly throughout the day. Locate this type of storage closest to the active work area.

- **Backup** - refill (bulk) items for active areas and items used occasionally during a typical week. Locate further away from the active work area but where easily accessible.

- **Long-term** - nonperishable, special-use and seasonal items. Use out-of-reach, back-of-the-building areas, under stairs and other less-accessible locations.

- **Protect employees from injury.** Place heavy items as close to waist height as possible. Provide sturdy step stools, ladders and rolling carts nearby. Except in rarely accessed areas, keep shelving shallow enough for easy reach. See the section "Creating Environments that Work with People."

- **Make storage cabinets in public areas attractive.** Make them a part of the décor. Use materials that clean easily.

- **Recapture additional space.** Clear out (toss, sell or trade in) fixtures, equipment or tools that haven't been used in the past 18-24 months.

- **Storage between deliveries.** Develop a list of dry and perishable foods that must be on hand to serve your average number of meals between deliveries. You will typically need enough space to store a two- to four-week supply of dry foods and one week or less of perishable foods.

- **Review your purchases.** Reassess purchases from a storage perspective. Base your review on availability (delivery frequency) and packaging (quantity and type). Remember, special order items, infrequent deliveries and high-usage products require greater storage capacity.

- **Create separate (but convenient) storage for chemical cleaners** and other hazardous materials. Check your local regulations regarding hazardous materials storage.

- **Evaluate all storage for potential cross-contamination issues.** This includes that of chemicals and foodstuffs as well as methods of handling these.

- **Incorporate easily movable or "sectional" storage** whenever possible to maximize layout flexibility.

Working (and Resting) Behind the Scenes

The kitchen isn't the only area where work has to be accomplished in order to run a successful restaurant. Think about the various non-food activities that your restaurant will perform: accounting, personnel, receiving and storing and other business functions. Here are some ideas for creating suitable support areas:

- **Office space.** Designate an area where cash can be counted, deposits made, checks written, employees interviewed and records stored. Figure out which tasks will be handled in this area before determining the amount of space required, the location and equipment needs.

- **Non-food storage areas.** Allocate a specific area for the handling of replacement china, flatware and tabletop accessories, along with seasonal decorations and catering/banquet/meeting equipment such as podiums and audiovisual equipment. Also, wood-burning fireplaces and ovens require significant space for wood storage.

- **Receiving area.** Create space for a designated "receiving area." It allows employees to count and inspect inbound shipments with minimum disruption. It is also easier in an open space to break down bulk items for quick and effective storage. Restaurants that provide delivery services or offer outside catering may also require a staging area.

Employee Rest Areas

A rest area for employees should consist of something more than a back step. Creating an employee-only area is a great way to tell your team how important they are to you and your operation. Some physical benefits you can provide for your employees include:

- **A place to rest their tired feet,** have a peaceful meal and take a shower or catch a quick nap before the next major rush.

- **Lockers** to secure their personal items and decorate with family pictures.

- **Employee-only lavatories** outfitted with personal necessities and medical supplies.

- **A communication center** with telephone for local calls, a daily paper, phone books and a bulletin board.

- **Break rooms** that can also handle new employee orientation, training sessions and other internal meetings.

The right equipment is vital.

CHAPTER EIGHT

EQUIPMENT

The Right Equipment for the Job

The excitement of getting new equipment, coupled with the legitimate desire to have the right tools, can be a stumbling block for unseasoned restaurant owners. Overspending or going heavily into debt for restaurant equipment puts a new business in a financial "hole" that isn't easy to overcome. Conversely, selecting poor quality or inadequate equipment can cost you significantly more in the long run than investing in the best piece of equipment for the job. To help you choose the right equipment, tools and utensils for food preparation, storage, dispensing and cleanup, you'll first need to consider the following issues:

- **How will I know what type of equipment I need?** Thumb through food service equipment catalogs. Look for capacity figures, energy ratings, materials used, and construction methods.

- **Hire an equipment specialist.** An experienced consultant is invaluable in equipment purchasing. He or she can handle the research, calculate life cycle costs, determine suitability and negotiate pricing on your behalf. Look for a food facilities designer in your area. Equipment dealers and manufacturers also have consultants to assist you. Beware of potential biases though; these people are ultimately salespeople.

- **Review your menu offerings, food service style and projected number of guests** in order to establish basic equipment needs and capacities:
    - Determine whether you need a dedicated piece of equipment or a multifunction unit.
    - Calculate capacity requirements.
    - Will you be able to deliver enough hot fries during lunch?
    - Will you need to purchase extra dishes or a faster dishwasher?
    - Compare purchasing prepared/preprocessed products against the cost of the necessary equipment, raw materials and labor costs to prepare your own.

- **Match equipment to your immediate needs.** Over-equipping your kitchen is a poor use of resources. Since growth isn't guaranteed and needs frequently change, don't overplan for the future. Better to use and depreciate equipment fully than to take a loss on resale or trade.

- **Visit the Foodservice Equipment Reports' site** at www.fermag.com for evaluations, manufacturer resources and buyer's guides.

Making Wise Equipment Purchases

Restaurant needs differ. But getting the best value for every dollar spent is a universal concern. Here are some helpful suggestions to ensure you get the necessary quality, service and performance out of your equipment:

- **Seek out recommendations.** Unfortunately, there is no Consumer Reports for restaurateurs. But asking peers, used equipment dealers, industry association members and food service equipment specialists can help you learn about desired features, life expectancies and brand names to consider or avoid.

- **Contact your local gas and/or electric utility company.** Many utility companies have fully outfitted test kitchens, where they promote gas or electric equipment from major manufacturers. Ask about available rebates and promotional programs.

- **Don't overlook custom-built equipment.** To get the quality, service and performance you need, the solution may be custom-built. This can be the best choice when: looks are important; you have unique specifications; or your usage exceeds the capacity of stock equipment.

- **Comparison shop.** Have your consultant or equipment dealer give you "good, better, best" recommendations. Compare features, operation costs and life expectancies.

- **Establish substitution rules.** Sometimes the equipment you select is not available due to excessive lead times, product discontinuation or unforeseen price increases. Carefully examine substitutions for suitability.

Look for commercial-grade materials and superior construction:
- Choose high-grade stainless with welded joints.
- Choose equipment doors that open away from the nearest worktable to facilitate removal of hot and heavy pans.
- Verify that the gauge of steel used is as quoted. Remember, the smaller the number, the thicker the steel.

- **Don't have equipment delivered until you are ready to install it.** Or you risk dents and dings. Dust can irreparably damage fragile equipment.

Which Quality Level?

Should I invest in the top brand on the market or purchase a serviceable low-end model? Who wouldn't want the latest and greatest in restaurant, office and business equipment? However, investing wisely and within your budget are both key contributors toward your long-term success.

Ask yourself the following decision-making questions:
- Does it fit within my budget?
- Would a smaller model save precious space?
- Will my food or service quality improve with this equipment?
- What is the ROI? For specialty equipment: Will I sell enough products or attract enough new customers to pay for it?
- Will it save energy costs, reduce overhead, or make employees more productive?
- Is it the most productive and energy-efficient equipment for the job?
- Is it difficult or expensive to operate daily?
- Will it be on display where looks are important?
- Does it meet sanitation, plumbing or building code requirements?
- What type of routine maintenance does it require?
- Is local service available and affordable?
- Is an economical service or maintenance contract available?
- Is the lifespan greater than the payment or lease terms?
- What's the resale value if I need to sell or tradeup?
- Are there trade-in/trade-up programs available?

Equipment Budgeting

The number one question asked is "How much should I spend?" Quality and pricing levels vary so widely that there is no easy answer. Successful restaurateurs tend to spend no more than they actually need. Consider the following:

- **Fit for purpose.** For some light-duty equipment, a less expensive, yet highly serviceable, brand may be the best choice. Alternatively, heavy use may require the best quality manufactured.

- **Keeping within budget**. Develop an equipment/ fixture/tool wish list. Divide your list into three priority categories: "Cannot Live Without", "Would Make Life Easier" and "Wouldn't It Be Great." Allocate your budget primarily to the first category. This is the equipment that makes you money. Review the items in category two for potential time and money savings. Be very objective about items in category three. Will the $14,000 espresso machine make a difference in your bottom line? Analyze your second and third category items for their potential return on investment.

- **Repayment.** Don't forget that all your equipment has to be paid for - eventually. Ask yourself how long it will take to pay for itself. Will it make you money or just make you look or feel better? Or, is leasing a wise alternative?

- **Review every decision from your CPA's viewpoint.** Buying cooking equipment can be like getting a new toy! Don't let your excitement or a salesperson's pitch eat up your budget.

- **Work closely with a food service consultant** or do your own research. Compare features and benefits to your acquisition and maintenance costs. Compare cost-per-year figures.

- **Negotiate for a better price.** Start by asking for 50 percent off the list price. Depending upon the equipment and the dealer's purchasing power, there is almost always some negotiation room.

- **Shop with major restaurant supply houses first.** Factory discounts to volume distributors could give you some additional negotiating room that isn't available with smaller suppliers.

- **Ask about last years' models.** Incentives may be available on older or overstocked models.

- **Check the Web for discounts.** Search under "restaurant equipment." Commercial equipment is frequently shipped directly from the manufacturer, so freight costs from a distant supplier may not be a factor. Ask whether they charge sales tax. This is a "gray" area for online purchases, and some states have no sales tax on restaurant equipment.

Equipment Leasing

For some restaurateurs, leasing can be a way to extend your available capital. Leasing is 100-percent financing. Depending on your lease, you may receive better tax benefits and lower monthly payments while preserving your working capital and borrowing capabilities. To help you determine which financing method suits your needs, here are some helpful ideas and resources:

- **Don't think of leasing as easy money.** The true cost of leased equipment can be much greater than the purchase price. You are paying "interest" even when you lease.

- **Avoid personal guarantees if possible.** If you sign it, you're liable even if your restaurant closes or the equipment doesn't last.

- **Educate yourself about leasing** before shopping for a leasing company. Leasing companies pull credit reports. Too many inquiries can negatively impact your credit report. Remain open-minded, however, and ask about used equipment leasing. This can be a cost-effective way to obtain top-quality equipment at reduced rates.

- **Confirm who is responsible for service and maintenance.** The manufacturer's warranty is extended to the lessee. However, in most cases, you are totally responsible for keeping the equipment in good working order and resalable condition.

- **Compare your total annual lease costs to your annual depreciation benefits.** Restaurant equipment has a seven-year depreciation rate as compared to that of a 36- to 60-month typical lease.

- **Don't lease items with a short life** or items that are fully deductible in the purchase year, such as flatware, glassware or dinnerware.

- **Be aware of leases with no or low buy-out provisions.** The IRS may classify it as a purchase agreement, subject to depreciation rules, instead of a 100 percent expense.

- **Insurance.** Make certain your insurance covers leased equipment adequately for fire, theft or other losses.

- **Get the fair-market-value information in writing.** Equipment with unrealistic residual values can have excessive buyouts. Check the used market for comparison figures.

- **Read the lease before signing.** A lease is a legal contract! You might even want your lawyer to review the fine print.

- **Estimate your monthly payments** and learn more about how leasing works from GE Leasing Solutions at www.geleasingsolutions.com.

Equipment Rental

Renting may be the solution for high-tech office needs, special occasions and for equipment with high maintenance costs, rapid obsolescence and low resale value. Renting, unlike leasing, is a straight month-to-month agreement with no potential ownership benefits, in which the rental company is responsible for service and maintenance. Some rentals are tied to the purchase of consumables, such as soft drinks, coffee, tea, detergents or printer ink. Before embarking upon equipment rental:

- **Understand the terms before signing** the rental agreement. The agreement should clearly detail the cancellation terms, who maintains ownership (this is important in communities where equipment is taxed), your maintenance/service responsibilities and the guaranteed level of service (will they repair it quickly?).

- **Watch out for the fine print and hidden costs!** Are you obliged to use only the rental company's supplies and consumables? Are you overpaying for these? Is there an accompanying minimum purchase requirement? Are the "extras" too costly? Are you prohibited from using competitive products?

- **Check close to home when renting.** Seek out local party stores, restaurant supply houses, catering supply specialists and Auto-Chlor System (60-year-old national dishwashing service).

- **Check your Yellow Pages.** Investigate such categories as office décor, computer systems, linens, restaurant equipment, telephones and dishwashing equipment.

Additional ideas and resources for renting décor, equipment and supplies. Consider renting:
- Indoor plants and aquariums.
- Commercial dishwashers.
- Portable refrigeration units.

- Beverage dispensers.
- Serving equipment (carts, warmers, carving stations).
- Seasonal décor.

Other reasons to consider renting:
- Your need is temporary.
- You'd like to "test drive" before buying.
- You want to change the décor regularly.
- You'd like to add something - a saltwater aquarium, for example, that requires regular expert care or rotating to look fresh.
- You don't want the maintenance hassles.
- You don't want the commitment of a lease.
- You don't want another capital expenditure.

Should I Buy Used Equipment/Fixtures?

Buying used restaurant equipment and fixtures can be a very wise decision. Just like those of a used car, equipment depreciation rates are greatest during the first year or two. Because of the unfortunately high failure rate in the restaurant business, there's always plenty of "almost-new" equipment available. Explore the following possibilities:

- **Before searching for a used piece of equipment, shop for new.** This will give you a benchmark of features, quality levels among manufacturers and pricing. Just as a used Mercedes is a safer investment than a used Yugo, so in restaurant equipment you should focus on top manufacturers with a reputation for quality.

- **Ask about the repair history of the make and model.** Institutional equipment typically has a long projected lifespan. Your dealer will probably have personal experience with the equipment.

- **Learn the terms "reconditioned" and "rebuilt."** "Reconditioned equipment" is cleaned, with worn/

broken parts replaced and a short dealer warranty, priced at 40-50 percent of new. "Rebuilt equipment" is totally dismantled and rebuilt, with a longer dealer warranty. It should provide performance equal to the manufacturer's specs and is priced at 50-70 percent of new.

- **Verify the equipment's age and history.** Use manufacturer's serial numbers and service records to check age and care. Don't rely on an "only driven on Sundays by Grandma" story.

- **Ask the used equipment supplier about their trade-in policy.** Some suppliers will give you above-average trade-in values when you return to purchase a new version.

- **Online.** Shop for used equipment online (auction and direct-purchase sites), at bankruptcy auctions, and from new equipment dealers and food equipment rep. groups.

- **Ask if they have demo models available.** Trade-show, showroom and test kitchen models can have a few "miles" on them and reduced, "scratch 'n dent" prices.

- **Save time by buying used.** Manufacturer's lead and delivery times on new equipment can be lengthy.

Don't buy:
- Cosmetically damaged equipment or fixtures that will be visible to customers.
- Anything with moderate (or worse) rust (except restorable cast iron).
- "Married" equipment (where the legs from one model have been attached erroneously to another model).
- Foreign-made equipment that wasn't made specifically for the U.S. market. Unknown electrical conversions can be a problem.

Equipment Suppliers

Your local restaurant equipment supply house is an obvious choice when shopping for commercial food service equipment. Here are some other sales outlets, suppliers and resources that you might consider when researching and shopping:

- **Food service equipment rep. groups.** These sales organizations represent a variety of manufacturers. Some only sell to distributors; others will sell direct.

- **Utility companies.** Your local gas or electric company may have a test kitchen outfitted by major manufacturers. You can "test drive" equipment, comparison shop and meet with factory reps here.

- **Web-based distributors.** Dozens of distributors have gone national with Web sites, such as:
  - Restaurant Equipment World at www.restaurantequipment.net
  - Independent Restaurant Equipment at www.food-equipment.com
  - Global Restaurant Equipment at www.global-restaurantequip.com

- **Procurement specialists.** Companies like ecFood at www.ecfood.com provide purchasing support. Many food service consultants also offer this specialty.

- **Auctions.** Local auction houses regularly liquidate the tangible assets of defunct commercial kitchens; however, only the Web offers 24/7 shopping and unsurpassed availability. Online auctions have become increasingly popular and offer vast "supplies" of all types of office and food service equipment and fixtures. Some sites also post local auction activities:
  - eBay at www.ebay.com and eBay Canada at www.ebay.ca

- Charyn Auctions at www.charynauctions.com
- Restaurant Auction at www.restaurantauction.com
- Able Auctions at www.ableauctions.com
- Check the Internet Auction directory at www.internetauctionlist.com for current online activity

Washing Dishware

Dishwashing is the "Rodney Dangerfield" of the kitchen. It gets no respect! What other restaurant activity is a major health concern, takes up so much space, costs so much and is only noticed when you don't do it right? Whether you serve meals in paper bags or on fine china, you'll have to wash something. Proper sanitation depends on a washing system that protects your customers while being efficient and cost-effective. Whether your establishment requires only a multisink configuration or you need the performance of a conveyor system, dishwashing decisions are important. Sanitation occurs when water, chemicals and heat are properly combined. Your basic needs in dishwashing are: waste removal, washing, sanitizing, rinsing and drying. Don't overlook the following:

- **Make certain your water pressure is ample** to operate your chosen commercial dishwasher. Poor water pressure may slow cycle times, inhibit automatic settings and not meet sanitation standards.

- **Calculate your water hardness.** Rinse aids may not be sufficiently effective without a separate water softener.

- **Review your hot water capacity and recovery times.** You'll need consistent temperatures of 150° F and above depending on your usage and your machine's capabilities.

- **Research low-temp dishwashing units** that use chemicals to sanitize and require lower water temperatures. Check with manufacturers such as Auto-Chlor Systems, Hobart and Champion for their recommended units.

- **Invest in a hot water booster.** Check with your local utility company regarding subsidies and rebates on select equipment.

- **Minimize cross-contamination, noise and unsavory smells.** Position dishwashing away from food prep and dining areas whenever possible.

- **Determine what you need to wash and when.** Will quick turnaround of expensive stemware require a separate glasswasher? Will you require a large storage area for soiled utensils or pots that are only handled after the rush is over? Will you have uniquely shaped equipment that will require soaking?

- **Consider what you'll need to wash off.** Lipstick stains on stemware? Grease on plastic?

- **Install a small undercounter glasswasher** in lounge/bar areas and front-of-the-house workstations. Also, install a low-flow (1.6 gpm) prerinse nozzle at your dishwashing station and save up to $100 a month in energy, water and sewer costs.

- **Non-automated washing.** In smaller operations or those with limited dish- or warewashing needs, a multisink configuration that complies with local regulations may be all you need. Be certain to:
  - Add ample counters and drain racks. Local codes dictate widths and lengths.
  - Separate dirty and clean dishware to avoid contamination.
  - Install a detergent dispenser to reduce waste.

- Maintain a consistent and high-enough water temperature by placing sinks near a dedicated water heater.

Commercial Dishwashers

Select the right dishwasher for the job. There are under-counter, standing (door) and conveyor models. Some are designed to handle a variety of dishware and larger pots; others are best suited to glassware and small items.

In choosing the right dishwasher, ask about:
- **Capacity.** The average number of place settings per hour. Estimate 90 to 110 settings per hour for a small- to medium-sized restaurant.

- **Water use.** Different manufacturers and models have different water needs. Compare gallons per load, water pressure and minimum temperatures. Some store and recirculate clean rinse water to minimize water waste.

- **Cycle times.** Time needed to wash and dry a load can range from 90 seconds to 3 minutes.

- **Dry method.** Can water spots or streaks be minimized? Will it require chemical rinse aids and/or water softeners?

- **Footprint.** Do you have enough space? Compare overall size to work capacity.

- **Openings and racks.** Can racks slide through easily? Do the doors open easily? Do you need a straight or corner configuration?

- **Ventilation.** Will additional ventilation be necessary?

- **Accessories.** How costly are additional racks?

- **Detergent requirements**. Compare the cost of recommended consumables (detergents, rinse aids).

- **Research equipment rental/chemical purchase programs.** The supplier owns and maintains the equipment. You pay a rental fee and purchase the supplier's chemicals. Auto-Chlor System, a well-known national supplier, can be found in your local Yellow Pages.

- **Create ample, convenient and secure storage (with no potential cross-contamination)** for chemical dishwashing agents. Rental/supply programs with monthly service require less chemical inventory.

- **Add a three-compartment sink in your dish room.** This is really useful for bulky or unusually shaped utensils and equipment components and as a backup for your commercial unit.

- **Stains.** Ask how specific stains or food residues, such as lipstick, eggs and grease, are removed.

Equipment-Specific Tips

Here are some purchasing tips on common heavy-use equipment.

- **Fryers.** Look for an insulated fry vat to reduce heat loss and idle energy use. Purchase units with solid-state temperature controls for precise temperatures. Investigate built-in filter systems to decrease oil costs and improve safety.

- **Water heaters.** Install quick-recovery booster water heaters for specific high-temperature needs. Insulate water heaters and all exposed pipes.

- **Ovens.** Visit your local test kitchen to compare standard ovens and convection ovens. Select programmable ovens for consistent quality of standard food offerings and reduced labor costs.

- **Pasta cookers.** Select the most energy-efficient model available, as boiling water is costly. Look for units with easy "idle" adjustments.

- **Broilers.** Be aware of costly and extensive venting requirements in some communities. Compare separate units (cheese melters and salamanders) to combination oven/broiler units.

- **Griddles.** Choose the right griddle for your menu: smooth or grooved. Investigate manufacturers that offer combo smooth/grooved griddles. Select the best quality steel plate you can afford for better energy efficiency.

- **Ranges.** Consider 30 kBtu/h open gas burners that produce more flame/flare for display kitchens. Explore induction cooking for quick-response cooktops. Caveat: flat-bottomed cookware is required for proper contact with the cooktop surface.

- **Braising pans.** Install a versatile braising pan (tilting skillet) to boil pasta, fry bacon or braise meat. This unit can be a cost-effective solution for busy kitchens.

- **Refrigerators.** Look for the EPA's Energy Star label for solid-door refrigerator/freezer units with an energy-savings payback of less than 1.5 years. To maximize a perishable's life, add separate units based on temperature needs. Some fruits and vegetables like it warmer and moister than dairy products. Make certain all walk-in units have safety systems to guard against accidental lock-ins.

- **Blast chiller.** Refrigeration units are engineered to store already-cool food. For added food safety, a blast chiller should be installed to reduce food temperatures in 120 minutes or less.

- **Ice machines.** Buy ample capacity. You'll need about 2 pounds of ice per dining room customer, 3 pounds in bars and about 1/2 to 2/3 the drink's weight in ice for self-service and take-out beverage units. Be certain that your ice machines/bins are not located near any heat source. Include a floor drain for maintenance and cleaning and provide nonskid rubber mats for safety.

- **Beverage dispensers.** Select longer levers or button operations for self-service soft drink units to minimize potential sanitation problems when customers refill. Look for units with removable tubes that can be cleaned easily and thoroughly.

- **Espresso machines.** Thoroughly research these, as this equipment can be difficult to maintain and repair. Since many units are made in Europe, ask how long the U.S. distributor has carried the product, and source a local repairperson before purchasing.

- **Mixers.** To determine required capacity, visit www.equipmentsystems.com/chart.htm. Select a mobile mixer to share among workstations. Be certain the mixer has ample horsepower for your task (mixing pizza, cookie or other heavy dough). Choose nonreactive stainless steel bowls for longer use. Add a timer to avoid overprocessing.

INDEX

If you enjoyed this book, order the entire series!

1-800-541-1336 Call toll-free
24 hours a day, 7 days a week.
Or fax completed form to:
1-352-622-5836. Order online!
Just go to **www.atlantic-pub.com**
for fast, easy, secure ordering.

Qty	Order Code	Book Title	Price	Total
	Item # RMH-02	THE RESTAURANT MANAGER'S HANDBOOK	$79.95	
	Item # FS1-01	Restaurant Site Location	$19.95	
	Item # FS2-01	Buying & Selling A Restaurant Business	$19.95	
	Item # FS3-01	Restaurant Marketing & Advertising	$19.95	
	Item # FS4-01	Restaurant Promotion & Publicity	$19.95	
	Item # FS5-01	Controlling Operating Costs	$19.95	
	Item # FS6-01	Controlling Food Costs	$19.95	
	Item # FS7-01	Controlling Labor Costs	$19.95	
	Item # FS8-01	Controlling Liquor, Wine & Beverage Costs	$19.95	
	Item # FS9-01	Building Restaurant Profits	$19.95	
	Item # FS10-01	Waiter & Waitress Training	$19.95	
	Item # FS11-01	Bar & Beverage Operation	$19.95	
	Item # FS12-01	Successful Catering	$19.95	
	Item # FS13-01	Food Service Menus	$19.95	
	Item # FS14-01	Restaurant Design	$19.95	
	Item # FS15-01	Increasing Restaurant Sales	$19.95	
	Item # FSALL-01	**Entire 15-Book Series**	**$199.95**	

Best Deal! SAVE 33%
All 15 books for $199.95

Subtotal	
Shipping & Handling	
Florida 6% Sales Tax	
TOTAL	

SHIP TO:

Name_____Phone(_____) _____

Company Name_____

Mailing Address _____

City _____State _____Zip _____

FAX _____E-mail _____

❏ My check or money order is enclosed   ❏ Please send my order COD   ❏ My authorized purchase order is attached

❏ Please charge my: ❏ Mastercard ❏ VISA ❏ American Express ❏ Discover

Card # ☐☐☐☐-☐☐☐☐-☐☐☐☐-☐☐☐☐   Expires ☐☐☐☐

Please make checks payable to: **Atlantic Publishing Company** • 1210 SW 23rd Place • Ocala, FL 34474-7014
USPS Shipping/Handling: add $5.00 first item, and $2.50 each additional or $15.00 for the whole set.
Florida residents PLEASE add the appropriate sales tax for your county.